T0284141

GOD IS...
ALL
You
NEED

GOD IS. . .
ALL
You
NEED

100 Devotions for Men

Elijah Adkins

BARBOUR
PUBLISHING

ISBN 979-8-89151-029-6

Published by Barbour Publishing, Inc., 1810 Barbour Drive, Uhrichsville, Ohio 44683, www.barbourbooks.com

Our mission is to inspire the world with the life-changing message of the Bible.

Member of the
Evangelical Christian
Publishers Association

Printed in China.

INTRODUCTION

God is all you need.

You've heard this statement in church and read it in devotional books. You probably agree wholeheartedly with the idea. But though it's a nice sentiment, what do these five words actually mean? Do you know *why* God is all you need? In what ways is God sufficient for you right now?

If you're not sure how to answer, that's okay. God has revealed the answers to such questions—and many, many more—in His Word. And this book is here to point you to those answers.

Together, we'll consider dozens of God's *attributes*—those qualities and characteristics that make Him who He is. Over the course of the following one hundred devotions, you'll learn about God—the amazing Trinity of Father, Son, and Holy Spirit—as

- » sovereign
- » omnipotent
- » forgiving
- » strong
- » faithful

- » wise

- » generous

- » "with us"

- » and much more.

You will see how these characteristics affect your life—today and through all eternity.

We'll dig into the theology of the Gospel of John and the apostle Paul's letter to the Ephesians, as well as the practical, day-by-day wisdom of books like James and Proverbs. In fact, we'll scan the breadth of scripture to learn more about the incredible God we serve. Everything we need to know about Him is right there in His Word, telling us exactly why He is all we need.

ETERNAL

*Before the mountains were brought forth or You
had ever formed the earth and the world, even
from everlasting to everlasting, You are God.*
PSALM 90:2

"All good things must come to an end."

Chances are, you've heard (and perhaps spoken) this cliché a hundred times. It's a modern proverb—a rough approximation of the "a time for everything" passage in Ecclesiastes—that's meant to offer a small degree of consolation in the face of a vanishing joy.

Only, it's not true. Sure, most good things *do* come to an end—your high school wonder years, for example, are behind you, as is the relaxing vacation you took last summer. And no matter how swell a day you're having now, it will be over in less than twenty-four hours. But as every Christian knows, there is one all-important exception to this sweeping rule: God.

Not only did God never begin, He will never end. Yet He exists all the same. Uncaused, unchanging, and unending, God is the single constant in this entropy-cursed universe. Even when all of material reality—from the largest galaxy to the dust beneath your feet—burns in divine fire at Judgment

Day, God will remain. And because of His love and your willingness to trust Him, you can remain by His side, sharing in the glory of His eternal nature.

In this life, all good things come to an end. But praise God, this life is only the beginning.

 **FOR FURTHER THOUGHT:**

Why is it so hard for us to grasp God's eternal nature? How can dwelling on this truth keep us from valuing earthly pleasures too much?

Everlasting God, I thank You for being my source of purpose. Help me never to hold too tightly to the treasures in this life. Unlike You, they were not meant to last.

OMNIPOTENT

"Alleluia. For the Lord God omnipotent reigns."
REVELATION 19:6

Today's verse includes one of the three "omnis," words that describe God's all-encompassing power, knowledge, and presence. In this case, *omnipotent* refers to God's power—His ability to perform any action, provided this action isn't inconsistent with the other attributes He possesses.

In fact, it's logically impossible to conceive of a more powerful being than God. Why? Because omnipotence isn't an attribute He gained through training; rather, it's a necessary attribute. Just as water is wet by definition, God is all-powerful by logical necessity.

When you truly consider the implications of such raw strength, you might find yourself on the verge of dizziness. *Stop the rotation of the earth?* No problem for God. *Create universes out of nothing?* Just a cozy Sunday afternoon activity for Him. *Defeat the power of sin and death?* Been there, done that.

So what should your response be to such a mind-shattering power? The answer is simple: trust. The moment you put your trust in an all-powerful God is the moment when all other powers, even the ones you fear and respect, fall prostrate before the one who controls them all. That daunting bill coming due next week, that pathology the doctor discovered in your body last month, and even the monstrous specter of death itself—all are governed by our omnipotent God.

You don't have to lean on your own power to combat life's forces. You serve power Himself, and He is more than willing to use that power to bring you to the place you need to be.

 **FOR FURTHER THOUGHT:**

Why do many Christian men believe in God's omnipotence yet still fear life's petty problems? What's the best cure for this cognitive dissonance?

Omnipotent Lord, teach me to trust Your power, even when a multitude of other powers are blocking my spiritual eyes.

OMNISCIENT

Great is our Lord and of great power;
His understanding is infinite.
PSALM 147:5

Our universe is a big, complex stew of information, spread out over billions of light years of space. It's so big, in fact, that a mathematician at Portsmouth University, Dr. Melvin M. Vopson, has calculated that the universe holds somewhere close to 7.5×10^{59} (that's 7.5 with 59 zeros!) zettabytes of information. For comparison, it is estimated that the total number of "zettabytes" of data produced globally in 2020 was a measly 64.2 (no zeros this time).

If your head is spinning, just wait until you hear the real shocker: God knows all of it.

In light of all that, it's easy to see why the psalmist used the word *infinite* to describe God's knowledge. For the man who doesn't follow God, this knowledge is terrifying. Hiding from God is not only ill-advised, it's absurd (see the book of Jonah). God knows our every action—even the ones we'd rather He never see.

But for the man who loves God and seeks to do His will, God's omniscience (His second "omni") is one of the most comforting facts in the universe. Not only does God see your struggles, He is also smart enough to arrange things so that they all work together for your good (Romans 8:28).

God is never taken by surprise, even when events happen that leave everyone else reeling in shock. Our reality is His chessboard, and God always wins.

 **FOR FURTHER THOUGHT:**

Have you ever tried hiding from God? What motivated that choice? What did you learn from that experience?

> *Omniscient God, how foolish it is to run from You or fear that You are somehow not aware of events in my life! Give me a proper understanding of Your infinite knowledge.*

OMNIPRESENT

Where shall I go from Your Spirit? Or where shall I flee from
Your presence? If I ascend up into heaven, You are there. If I
make my bed in hell, behold, You are there. If I take the wings
of the morning and dwell in the uttermost parts of the sea, even
there Your hand shall lead me and Your right hand shall hold me.

PSALM 139:7–10

Omnipresence, God's third and final "omni," is where things start getting confusing. How can God be in two places (or ten or ten trillion) at the same time? Does this mean He's spread out like some sort of cloud, infusing all creation with bits and pieces of Himself? Or is it like pantheism, which teaches God simply *is* everything?

Neither.

God's entire presence is in every location at once. All of Him is present where you are now, and all of Him will be present in your room tonight when you shut your eyes in sleep.

It's not hard to think of why this matters to us. Whenever you're having a terrible day—when your boss chews you out, a tree falls on your garage, or a close friend stabs you in the back—it's always nice to have someone present. God is that someone. When you're tempted to respond to these inconveniences in unhealthy ways, it's great to remember someone is right there, holding you accountable. God is that someone. And when you fall so hard that you feel cut off from dignity itself, it's comforting to know someone is willing to welcome you back with open arms. God is that someone.

Wherever you are, God is there also, willing to make Himself known. . .but only if you're willing to see Him.

 **FOR FURTHER THOUGHT**:

How should God's omnipresence affect our behavior? How often do you think of God's presence whenever you're facing a challenge?

Omnipresent Lord, remind me of Your presence whenever I feel You're far away.

LOVE

He who does not love does not know God, for God is love.
1 JOHN 4:8

If all we knew about God were the previous four attributes, we might have reason to be a bit frightened. After all, an eternal, all-powerful, all-knowing, all-present being is not the kind of entity you'd want to encounter if you thought He wasn't kind and good.

But thanks to today's verse (and countless others like it) we know that God *is* kind and good. In fact, not only is He benevolent and compassionate toward His wayward creation, He is intensely in love with us unlovable creatures. He loves us so much that He was willing to wrap His glorious essence in mortal flesh and, in order to rescue us from our own prison of sin and shame, suffer the most shameful and painful death imaginable.

Thanks to Jesus' actions on the cross, we now have an idea of what perfect love looks like: Him.

This is wonderful news, and we have the responsibility of spreading that news to everyone. Not only that, we are called to emulate this love in our interactions with others. God, after all, doesn't play favorites—He loves each one of us equally, so as His children, we should practice loving our friends, enemies, and neighbors equally as well.

Is your life filled with proof that you know the God of love?

 FOR FURTHER THOUGHT:

Is it possible to ever reach God's level
of love? When can we stop trying?

*Loving God, thank You for loving me to
a degree I'll never be able to understand.
Teach me how to model my life after the
love that comes so naturally to You.*

JUST

"For I, the LORD, love justice."
ISAIAH 61:8

"You can't criticize me; I'm just living out my truth."

How often have you heard this statement, or some variant of it? It's a fairly popular refrain in our postmodern society—a chorus sung to the baffling tune "Subjective Morality." Now, however, this chaos of moral relativism is giving way to a more sinister—but equally arbitrary—system of ethics. Having understood the absurdity of a life without a solid system of morality, the culture is starting to embrace once again a shared set of moral laws.

The problem? Society has created these laws themselves. It's subjective morality all over again—but this time with a new coat of paint.

Without God as the ultimate standard for justice, the laws of civilization will constantly be in flux, tearing society apart from within. Everyone innately recognizes the importance of absolute truth (Romans 1:18–19), but it seems people cannot agree on the source of this truth. Therefore, our supposedly enlightened culture is regressing into a state of primitivism, in which everyone does what is right in his own eyes (Judges 17:6).

But since God *is* our standard for justice—and will be at the end of time—the church doesn't have to follow the world's path of moral decay. Rather, we should continue living by His laws, serving as a compass for this directionless world.

Justice is part of God's nature. Is it part of yours?

 **FOR FURTHER THOUGHT:**

In what ways have many Christians bought into the idea of subjective morality? How damaging do you think this line of thinking will be in the long run?

> *Lord of justice, You alone hold the keys of right and wrong. Teach me to appeal to You— not my own misguided sense of justice— as the source of every judgment I make.*

PERFECT

As for God, His way is perfect.
PSALM 18:30

Some people are perfectionists. Whenever they notice a misplaced book on the coffee table or a spot of dust on the floor, they're on it in a heartbeat. The perfectionist has to tidy things up to make his living quarters exactly how he sees them in his head.

Now, compare that to today's scripture. God isn't a perfectionist in the sense of Him striving toward an impossible ideal. No, He is already at this point of perfection, and He has been for eternity. He has no failings. He governs His creation with meticulous accuracy, and He governs His own actions with a perfect will. Everything He does is entirely intentional and indisputably *right*. Any flaw or imperfection we might think we see in God inevitably boils down to a flaw in our own spiritual eyesight.

Even though it is impossible for us to live up to His standard of perfection, Jesus tells us we should still try (Matthew 5:48). Why? Is it because God wants us to impress Him with our decidedly unimpressive attempts? No—one reason is that whenever we look to God as our standard of perfection, we begin reflecting small shimmerings of His light toward those who otherwise might never see Him. Another reason is simply because we are His children—and nothing pleases a father more than when his children try to imitate him.

There's nothing wrong with being a spiritual perfectionist. Just never forget that God is both the goal and the power that drives all your efforts.

 FOR FURTHER THOUGHT:

How can a Christian man overcome frustration
whenever perfection seems out of reach?
Do you see perfection as a desirable goal?

*Perfect God, give me a burning desire to reach out
toward Your perfection. I know I'll never attain it,
but I want to get as close to You as I can in all I do.*

JUDGE

*I charge you therefore before God and the Lord
Jesus Christ, who shall judge the living and the
dead at His appearing and His kingdom.*
2 TIMOTHY 4:1

Earlier, we talked about God's justice—the fact that He is our
only true standard of right and wrong. Logically, this means
God is the only one who has the right to judge humanity.

Ironically, many people misuse this fact as a way to take
the heat off themselves because of their sinful lifestyle. "Only
God can judge me," they say, not taking into account that
today's verse says that is exactly what He intends to do.

For many people, the knee-jerk reaction to the truth that
Christ will be our judge might be terror or dread. After all,
Hebrews 10:31 says, "It is a fearful thing to fall into the hands
of the living God." But keep in mind: if you are trusting
Jesus as Savior, if you are putting your faith in the sin-
cancelling sacrifice He made for you, then you don't have to
worry about "falling" into God's hands. God already has you
in His hands—to protect you, not to destroy you.

But for those who don't know God or are fleeing His
presence, today's verse is as terrifying as they come. Sinners
will not be able to argue their way out of God's judgment

or obfuscate the evidence. God's decree will be perfect and everlastingly final (Matthew 3:12); there will be no second chances (Hebrews 9:27).

When that day comes, which side of God's judgment will you be on?

🔆 FOR FURTHER THOUGHT:

Why is judgment such an unpopular concept in today's world? Why must the church never abandon this doctrine, even when it feels uncomfortable?

> *Righteous judge, fill me with concern for those who don't know You. I want everyone to accept Your forgiveness before it's too late.*

SELF-SUFFICIENT

"For as the Father has life in Himself, so He has given to the Son to have life in Himself."
JOHN 5:26

This verse says God has "life in Himself." What does that mean?

Well, consider the life that humanity possesses. Where did that life originate? Genesis 2:7 says it was "breathed" into mankind by God. And after that, humanity has lived on food, water, and oxygen—all of which were created by God.

So where did God's life originate? Who "breathed" life into Him?

No one. His life was already within Him before the universe was made—before time itself began. In fact, continuous existence is another one of God's fundamental attributes. He does not require oxygen or food to keep living: His existence is written in the laws of logic itself. In no possible reality does God *not* exist. Just as two plus two will always equal four, God will always have life in Himself.

This has staggering implications for how a Christian man should live. The most obvious thing it should do is erase pride altogether, replacing it with thankfulness and surrender. Nothing you do is done by yourself—it all comes back to

God. Everything from your career to your car to your house to the air you're breathing right now originates with Him, the source of all power and existence.

Given this information, absolute reliance on Him is the only rational plan of action. Just as a clear-thinking man would never lock himself in a vacuum to see if he can survive without breathing, so a true Christian would never break away from God, the source of our sufficiency.

 **FOR FURTHER THOUGHT:**

Do you sometimes live like you're self-sufficient? In what ways would this be offensive to God?

> *Lord, I'm humbled by the thought of Your self-sufficiency. Teach me never to look inward for the purpose and power that can only be found in You.*

HOLY

"Holy, holy, holy, is the Lord of hosts.
The whole earth is full of His glory."
ISAIAH 6:3

As fallen humans living in a fallen world, it's difficult to wrap our minds around the definition of the word *holy*.

Leviticus 20:26, however, gives us a clue. God says to the Israelites, "You shall be holy to Me, for I the Lord am holy and have set you apart from other people, that you should be Mine." Holiness, therefore, carries with it the idea of separation and distinctness. God is separate and distinct in every way from sinful human beings. There is absolutely nothing that compares to Him in all His creation.

Because God is holy, we are to treat Him as such, expressing reverence when entering His presence and keeping Him first in our lives. The moment we start blending God's holiness with the world's mundane imperfection is the moment we've replaced God with an inferior lookalike in our hearts.

Because of God's holiness, the Old Testament is filled with warnings against approaching God improperly. Uzzah touched the ark of the covenant—the physical symbol of God's presence—and died on the spot (2 Samuel 6:6–7).

Similarly, the children of Israel could not approach Mount Sinai when God was there; otherwise, they would be subject to execution (Exodus 19:12).

But thanks to Jesus' sacrifice, God's holiness is no longer a barrier between us and His presence. Rather, it's an attribute that God invites us to share in and enjoy (1 Thessalonians 5:23)—a path that traverses His once-forbidden mountain.

Are you climbing that path today?

 **FOR FURTHER THOUGHT**:

Does the thought of God's holiness frighten or comfort you? Why? How can a Christian maintain a proper attitude toward God's holiness?

Holy God, thank You for becoming accessible to all who seek You. May I never treat Your holiness flippantly, however. I want Your name to be separate from all others in my heart.

SOVEREIGN

The lot is cast into the lap, but the decision-making is of the Lord.
PROVERBS 16:33

Imagine this scenario: You're at home in your pajamas, watching a riveting football game on television. Your team is down by five, and only twenty seconds remain on the clock. The star running back has the ball, and he's driving it down the field like a bulldozer.

"You can do it!" you scream at the screen, focusing all your mental energy onto the ball, trying to will it down the field like some sort of sports-crazed Jedi. The ball crosses the goal line as the clock reaches 00:00. You applaud, then exhale in relief, pleased that you contributed to your team's victory.

Wait. . .what?

Believe it or not, this irrational attitude is fairly common. Psychologists call it the illusion of control, and it manifests itself whenever a desired outcome becomes reality—even though the guy watching the game played absolutely no part in bringing it about.

God, however, is subject to no such illusions. He is simply in control. Full stop. From every star that explodes in the distant heavens to every snowflake that settles gently in your backyard, God has timed each event to perfection. We may attribute outcomes to chance, superstition, or our own abilities, but the only true cause resides with God—reality's sovereign ruler.

So today, replace your "illusion of control" with a solid trust in the God who truly controls it all.

 **FOR FURTHER THOUGHT:**

Why are people tempted to take credit for things
they could never have foreseen, let alone controlled?
How does God's sovereignty impact your view of life?

> *Sovereign Lord, may I never take credit for the things You have accomplished. I could never handle the pressure of being in control anyway.*

CREATOR

In the beginning God created the heaven and the earth.
GENESIS 1:1

"Whatever begins to exist has a cause."

Argue with it, deny it, or explain it away all you want, this statement—a form of the cosmological argument for God's existence—is one of the fundamental truths of reality. And as modern science increasingly points to the biblical truth that the universe had a beginning, it becomes more and more illogical to deny the existence of a Creator.

To understand the extent of God's creativity, it's helpful to look at all the things He has made: the air you breathe, the water you drink, the carbon molecules that comprise your body, the planet you walk on, the space through which this planet hurtles at thousands of miles per hour, the flow of time that permits motion itself, and the mind that lets you ponder all these amazing proofs of God's power.

From the cosmic to the mundane, God is the Creator. This is His universe; we're just living in it.

What are we to do with this information? Well, start by thanking Him and taking precautions to preserve the things He has made. Then consider the fact that since we are made in God's image, we too have the urge to create. Humanity strives to create order out of chaos, to build grand structures and create beautiful works of art, and to carve out for themselves a beautiful, meaningful life. All such endeavors are admirable, especially when they are done for the glory of God.

He is the ultimate Creator. How are you using the creativity He's given you to glorify His name?

 **FOR FURTHER THOUGHT:**

How often do we take for granted the fact that all our resources were created by God? How can a Christian keep from forgetting God's role as Creator?

Almighty Creator, thank You for this beautiful world. Help me to accomplish my role as steward, using my resources and abilities to point others to Your power.

SUSTAINER

O LORD, You preserve man and beast.
PSALM 36:6

In our minds, God's role as sustainer may take a back seat to His role as Creator. This is understandable—after all, the spontaneous creation of a universe from nothing is a lot more impressive to us than the behind-the-scenes work with which God is consistently engaged.

But Hebrews 1:3 gives us a brief glimpse into God's work of preservation when it describes Him as "upholding all things by the word of His power." This is present tense—a description of an ongoing work that, if it were to cease, would spell the immediate destruction of time and space.

Needless to say, this understanding should greatly increase our appreciation of the world we inhabit. God is not obliged to keep upholding this universe any more than He was to create it in the first place. In fact, it's incredible to think He would ever choose to uphold it, given the human corruption that runs deep within the heart of His creation.

And yet He still does. Why?

Because as 2 Peter 3:9 eloquently says, God is "not willing that any should perish but that all should come to repentance." He loves us so much that He is willing to keep this show running for those who are still unwilling to obey Him. One day, time will run out (verse 10). But for now, God sustains our lives so that we can surrender those lives to Him.

What is your response to God's sustaining power?

 FOR FURTHER THOUGHT:

Which do you find more amazing: God's creative power or His sustaining power? Does either one require more energy for Him to perform? Why or why not?

Lord, sustainer of all things, teach me to live as if this day is my last. I never want to take this time You have given me for granted.

PATIENT

May the God of patience and consolation grant you to be like-minded toward one another, according to Christ Jesus.
ROMANS 15:5

Given that God is the sustainer of all things—despite the fact that humanity's sinfulness gives Him every reason *not* to sustain all things—we can easily deduce another important attribute of God: His patience.

Second Peter 3:8 says, "Beloved, do not be ignorant of this one thing, that one day with the Lord is as a thousand years, and a thousand years as one day." As the nameless eons of history slip by, God watches, patiently waiting for His plan to reach its fulfillment. To us mortals, such lengths of time are incomprehensible—frightening, even. To God, however, these stretches of history are no more imposing than a thirty-second microwave timer is to us. But maybe that's a bad analogy—many of us have problems even with that!

Whenever we're in the middle of heartbreak or enduring a painful season of illness or loss, we can forget that God is much more patient than we are. *Maybe God just gave up and walked away*, you might think. *How could this be part of His plan?*

Rest assured—God has not gone anywhere. Even when

you feel frustrated by the slow-moving gears of Providence, you can take consolation that God is running the machine at exactly the right speed. You might never reach God's level of patience (how could you?), but a good understanding of His nature goes a long way toward making this life a more rewarding journey.

FOR FURTHER THOUGHT:

Why do you think God has no problem waiting for His plan to reach fulfillment? How can a Christian man grow in patience?

Ever-patient God, thank You for taking the time to ensure that my life reaches the place You want it to be. Without Your patience, I would have been a lost cause long ago.

FATHER

*Behold, what manner of love the Father has bestowed
on us, that we should be called the sons of God.*

1 JOHN 3:1

According to the US Census Bureau, 17.8 million children live in fatherless homes throughout the United States. That's roughly a quarter of children nationwide. As the National Fatherhood Initiative somberly notes, that's enough kids to fill Los Angeles four times over.

It doesn't take a list of statistics to illustrate how detrimental this is, but perhaps a few would help. Roughly 90 percent of runaway children, 85 percent of youths in prison, 71 percent of high school dropouts, and 60 percent of young suicide victims all share one thing in common—the lack of a father in the home.

Today's verse, however, offers hope. By sending Jesus, His Son, to reconcile this earth to Himself, God broke the barrier between us, enabling a closely knit Father-child relationship that had previously been impossible. And our heavenly Father is nothing like a non-custodial parent. Jesus taught in Matthew 7:9–11 that God is always present, ready to dole out the best gifts for His children when they ask.

Whether or not your childhood home lacked a father,

it's never too late to embrace God as your heavenly Father. And if you have children (or plan to someday), you can follow God's example so that your kids will never have to know what it means to live in a fatherless home.

 FOR FURTHER THOUGHT:

In what ways is God different than even the best fathers on earth? Do you see God as a distant authority or as a loving dad?

Heavenly Father, I'm not sure where I would be if You were absent from my life. Thank You for adopting me as Your son and loving me as only You can.

SON

And the high priest answered and said to Him, "I adjure You by the living God, that You tell us whether You are the Christ, the Son of God." Jesus said to him, "You have said it."
MATTHEW 26:63–64

Just as God is the Father, so He also is the Son. Don't worry—we'll soon dive more deeply into that topic and all the mysteries it entails. For now, just know that Jesus, who is God, is also the Son of God and that He came to earth to fulfill His role as the obedient child of the Most High.

Hebrews 5:8 says, "Though [Jesus] was a Son, He learned obedience by the things that He suffered." This is not to say Jesus lacked perfection and somehow had to get to that point. Rather, it means that just as a son learns what is right and wrong through his father's discipline, so Jesus' willingness to obey was consistently honed—not weakened—by the rejection and humiliation and eventual crucifixion He faced. He did this not by relying on the strength of His human body or mind but by receiving strength directly from His all-powerful Father (John 5:19).

Are you such a son? You'll never experience the trauma that Jesus faced, but you'll most assuredly come to a point in which your own strength just isn't enough.

In that moment, you'll need your Father's power coursing through your veins, strengthening your will to obey.

 FOR FURTHER THOUGHT:

If God the Father and God the Son are equal in their deity, why did one choose to submit to the other? How obedient are you to your Father?

Lord Jesus, thank You for taking on the role of obedient Son so that I can become an adopted son of the almighty God. Teach me how to obey as You did.

SPIRIT

"God is a Spirit, and those who worship Him
must worship Him in spirit and in truth."

JOHN 4:24

Throughout the Bible, God's existence as a Spirit is repeatedly confirmed. The second verse of Genesis says God's Spirit was present at creation, hovering over the face of the primordial deep. Second Peter describes the ancient prophets as "holy men of God [who] spoke as they were moved by the Holy Spirit" (1:21). And in the final chapter of scripture, God and His church are elegantly described as "the Spirit and the bride" (Revelation 22:17).

But what exactly is a spirit? Well, the Bible doesn't give a concrete answer, but it does give us enough information to form an educated guess. We know, for instance, that we all have a spirit. . .and that when we die, it leaves the body to be with God (Genesis 25:8, 35:29; Matthew 27:50; Ecclesiastes 3:21). Based on that information, we can assume a spirit isn't bound by the laws of nature; rather, it is something immaterial and immortal. When you strip away everything that describes you—your body, your brain, your personality—what's left is your spirit. In other words, your spirit is *you*.

Since God is a Spirit, you'll never be able to see Him with

your natural eyes. Instead, as today's verse says, you commune with Him spirit to Spirit—your spirit to His.

Your body shouldn't just go through the motions of worshipping God; worship Him from the essence of your being—with all your heart and spirit.

 **FOR FURTHER THOUGHT:**

Even though we are spirit at our core, why is it so hard to understand what a spirit is? Do you regularly engage in spirit-to-spirit conversations with God?

Holy Spirit, I need Your presence in my life. Teach me how to worship You the way I should—"in spirit and in truth."

TRINITY

"Therefore go and teach all nations, baptizing them in the name of the Father and of the Son and of the Holy Spirit."
MATTHEW 28:19

For the uninitiated (and even for many longtime believers), today's verse is something of an enigma. There is one God, right? So why are three names listed here? Are these simply three "modes" in which God operates—sort of like the way water can be liquid, solid, or gas?

No, because as we've already learned, Jesus the Son was obedient to God the Father, and He regularly prayed to His Father for guidance and strength. Also, Jesus spoke of the Holy Spirit as separate from Himself (Luke 12:10), implying there is a total of three distinct persons being referenced in scripture. As for how this remains true alongside the truth that God is one—don't worry, we'll get there. For now, just know that God exists as three persons—Father, Son, and Holy Spirit—the Trinity.

So what does this mean for us? Is this just an academic exercise designed to confuse theology students? No, knowledge of the Trinity can benefit us in two ways: First, it gives us a better appreciation for how the plan of salvation operates—the Father sent the Son as a sacrifice, and the Son provides the Holy Spirit to indwell us believers (John 20:22). Second, it helps us understand that God, being so much higher than we, will always be full of surprises. Nobody could have guessed that God exists as a Trinity, so who are we to imagine we have Him all figured out?

Today, embrace the mystery of our tri-personal God.

 FOR FURTHER THOUGHT:

How does God's attribute as a Trinity help
prove that the ancients couldn't have simply
"made Him up" in their minds? How often
have you thought of God's triune nature?

> *Triune God, thank You for revealing
> portions of Your great mystery to us.*

ONE

"Hear, O Israel: The LORD our God is one LORD."
DEUTERONOMY 6:4

Christians throughout history have offered models for how God's oneness squares with His nature as three persons. From the common (but faulty) "water analogy" mentioned in yesterday's reading to the early church fathers' illustration of God as the sun (with the Father the physical sun, Jesus its rays, and the Holy Spirit the heat), each model attempts to explain the inexplicable. As a result, no matter how close these analogies get to the truth, they will never fully encapsulate God's mysterious nature.

Each person of the Trinity *is* God—not just a part of Him. As Colossians 2:9 implies, "the fullness of the Godhead" is contained in each member of the Trinity. And today's verse explains that there is only one God—not three of them. God *is* the Son, the Father, and the Holy Spirit, yet these three persons are decidedly distinct.

Therefore, Christianity is not some hybrid form of polytheism, as some mistakenly assume. Rather, it rests on the foundation of a single, almighty God who lies beyond the threshold of our limited human experience yet who loves us enough to cultivate a relationship with each of His children.

And the longer we stay in this relationship, the more we'll discover who God truly is.

 FOR FURTHER THOUGHT:

Why do you think God created us with limited understanding? How can mysteries about God's nature actually draw us closer to Him?

God, You are one Lord, and I come before You humbled by Your singular might and majesty. Thank You for utilizing each aspect of Yourself to bring about my salvation.

UNCHANGING

"I am the LORD; I do not change.
Therefore you sons of Jacob are not consumed."
MALACHI 3:6

Have you ever had a friend who seemed a bit. . .unhinged? Maybe he'd sit down and chat with you about basketball and politics one day but not even return your "hello" the next day. Every time you approached him, you'd wonder inwardly, *Which person will he be today?*

Truthfully, we're all like that sometimes. Perhaps you don't notice this behavior in yourself, but that's only because you are perfectly aware of all the factors that cause you to behave differently in the presence of others—a bad day at work, a promotion, an argument with your wife—while nobody else has a clue. They may walk away thinking, *Wow, what's his problem?* while you are unaware that you just behaved like your unpredictable friend.

In short, we change. We're always changing. It's part of our nature. God, however, does not change. His attributes are as immovable as the laws of logic. That's why you can open a book that was written thousands of years ago by many different authors and still trust it to hold true today.

The world might want a God who changes with the

times, but thankfully, our God is not that kind of God. If He were, who's to say He would change on our behalf? A changing God would be a fickle tyrant, leaving His creation in fear of what unpredictable mood He might possess today. Instead, our God's law and His love both stand true forever.

You can confidently follow this unchanging God.

 **FOR FURTHER THOUGHT:**

In what ways does modern culture want God to change? Why must the Christian never compromise when it comes to God's unchanging commands?

> *Unchanging Lord, keep me from becoming swept away by my culture's changing tide. You alone are the source of truth, now and for all time.*

REWARDER

Without faith it is impossible to please Him, for he who comes to God must believe that He is, and that He is a rewarder of those who diligently seek Him.
HEBREWS 11:6

Earlier, we spoke of God's role as judge. But while the word *judge* has connotations of punishment, today's verse reveals the other side of God's sense of justice: His willingness to reward His saints.

Notice that this reward doesn't come to those who merely try to improve their lives or those who behave better than the bottom rung of society. No, it comes to "those who diligently seek Him." Why? Because God recognizes the fact that we have no righteousness in ourselves—so He gives us credit we don't deserve whenever we seek His righteousness instead.

God is not a tyrant. He is not even an overbearing parent. Rather, He is the God of pure love and compassion who knows how hard it is for us to keep our heads straight in this earthly labyrinth.

Some days, you'll feel like you're on top of the world—like you have everything figured out and all will be right forever. Still, on those days it's your responsibility to ignore your pride and to diligently seek Him. Other days, you'll feel so far away from God that His light appears dimmer than the most distant star. On those days, it's your responsibility to ignore your emotions and likewise to diligently seek Him.

You do the seeking, and God will do the finding. That's just what He does.

 **FOR FURTHER THOUGHT:**

What are some ways a Christian can seek God? How diligently are you seeking Him? Are you willing to be found?

> *Lord, I am sometimes so confused in this life that I can't tell right from wrong. Thank You for giving me a simple command—to seek You. May I never ignore or disobey it.*

MERCIFUL

*Praise the LORD. O give thanks to the LORD,
for He is good, for His mercy endures forever.*
PSALM 106:1

In one episode of *The Andy Griffith Show*, Sheriff Andy Taylor must leave the cozy town of Mayberry for a single day to attend to matters elsewhere, so he temporarily hands the town over to his bumbling, overzealous deputy Barney Fife. Andy returns to find Barney sitting smugly behind the sheriff's desk, with practically every citizen of Mayberry locked up in the jail cells beside him.

Barney had done everything so perfectly, following every nuance expressed in the law, that absolutely nobody—not even the mayor or the unassuming Aunt Bee—had escaped his critical eye.

In a way, we're all like those hapless citizens of Mayberry when it comes to our own righteousness. Romans 3:23 says, "All have sinned and come short of the glory of God." And what are the consequences of sin? Well, they are a lot more severe than an overnight stay in a county jailhouse (see Romans 6:23).

God, however—being much more merciful than the floundering Barney Fife—has so arranged it that those who trust in the sacrifice made by His Son will escape the punishment they deserve. This offer of mercy extends from the moment we as children gain the ability to understand the gospel to the moment we breathe our last—a whole lifetime of mercy.

And for those who accept it, this mercy will continue on till the end of time. . .and from there, onward to forever.

 FOR FURTHER THOUGHT:

How can a Christian man enjoy the benefits of God's mercy without taking His mercy for granted? Are you showing mercy to the people in your life, just as God has shown mercy to you?

Merciful God, thank You for giving me blessings I don't deserve—and for sparing me from the punishment I do.

SHEPHERD

The LORD is my shepherd. I shall not want.
PSALM 23:1

Being called a sheep isn't usually considered a good thing, and it's easy to see why—sheep are pretty dull creatures. A popular internet video shows a sheep being rescued from a narrow crevice in the ground, only to run immediately in a semicircle and jump headlong into the same crevice.

Without a shepherd to guide them, sheep will inevitably get lost—or worse, get themselves killed. They seem practically brainless, so they need the brains of another to get by. That's why in today's culture of political agendas and misinformation, words like "sheeple" have become shorthand for those who reflexively obey orders from the top, never following the strength of their own convictions.

For a twenty-first-century Christian, the fact that today's verse implicitly compares believers to sheep might be a bit off-putting. But notice the distinction: *God* is our shepherd, not some government agency or questionable internet news source. We're not receiving our facts and guidance from a late-night talk show host or the local conspiracy theorist. We get real truth from the author of all truth. So when God says we should take an action or live a certain way, we don't have to hesitate or check His sources. Instant obedience is our only rational course of action.

God wants to be our shepherd. Are you willing to be His sheep?

 **FOR FURTHER THOUGHT:**

How does God's status as shepherd impact your life?
Is the idea of being a sheep embarrassing or not? Why?

> *Good shepherd, I place my trust in every*
> *word You speak. Teach me to follow You,*
> *without question or hesitation, into the green*
> *pastures You have prepared for Your sheep.*

FRIEND

"You are My friends if you do whatever I command you."
JOHN 15:14

How many friends do you have?

With the advent of social media, what was once a simple question has become muddled. The word *friend*, once an emotionally rich term that spoke of deep bonds between spiritual brothers and sisters, has become all but meaningless. A man can have hundreds of friends—thousands, even—and yet not really know a single one of them. In fact, many of his "friends" may actually be A.I. bots that sent him a request on Facebook three years ago and have been quietly gleaning and selling his information ever since.

But that's not the kind of friend Jesus is. His relationship with us reaches beyond the bounds of earthly acquaintances and friends—in fact, He "is a friend who sticks closer than a brother" (Proverbs 18:24).

Don't get confused—the Trinity of God the Father, Jesus the Son, and the Holy Spirit is not our equal. There is an undeniable aspect of reverence and respect that must be involved in our friendship with Him, as seen in today's verse. Yet this relationship is also so much more than a mere master-servant bond. God is not in our lives simply to boss us around. He is willing to share in our emotions and pain, taking us by the hand and guiding us to the place where we can live with Him forever.

 **FOR FURTHER THOUGHT:**

Is God your closest friend? Are your friendships modeled after the friendship God has with you? That is, are you gracious, compassionate, and helpful?

Lord, thank You for being my friend in this lonely world. May I never forget to cultivate this friendship each chance I get—whether that's through prayer or reading Your Word.

THE WAY

*Jesus said to him, "I am the way, the truth, and the life.
No man comes to the Father except through Me."*
JOHN 14:6

Today's verse gives us three of Jesus' attributes at once. We'll go through them one by one, starting with the first—Jesus is the way.

While many church leaders and religious experts have adopted an "all roads lead to Rome" mentality when it comes to faith, today's verse clearly states that Jesus is the only way to God.

Sure, God can use a variety of methods to lead people to Him—everything from their personal backgrounds to tragedies to great triumphs can be tools He uses to draw a person closer to salvation. But when speaking of the means by which a person can enter into a relationship with God, Jesus is the only route.

The world will call this message too exclusive. In reality, it's anything but. It's a revolutionary call that extends not just to the rich or the pious but to the poor and the irreverent, from the social elite to the social outcast, from presidents and kings to the twisted souls who inhabit their prisons. Anyone can, at any time, reach out and grab Jesus' hand.

But just as roads don't magically appear beneath a person's feet, so we're all personally responsible for choosing the path to Jesus as our Savior.

His sacrifice paved the way of salvation for the whole world. Are you walking Jesus' narrow way today?

 **FOR FURTHER THOUGHT:**

Why is it tempting to claim there are other ways to heaven? If this were true, how would it make Jesus' sacrifice ultimately meaningless?

Lord God, may I never be so arrogant as to try inventing new ways to heaven. Jesus is the way, so that's the way I am going to walk.

THE TRUTH

Jesus said to him, "I am the way, the truth, and the life.
No man comes to the Father except through Me."
JOHN 14:6

Have you ever met someone who believes truth doesn't exist? Perhaps you've seen this sentiment expressed in the form of an internet meme that shows two people looking at a number written on the ground. One person says, "This number is a six," while the other says from the opposite viewpoint, "No, it's a nine." The implication being, of course, that neither are correct or incorrect—it's all just a matter of perspective, so any arguments over the subject are useless.

But that's where the logic starts getting muddled. After all, this number didn't just appear on the ground—someone had to have written it with a specific value in mind. The number isn't a random scribble. It possesses an objective meaning that's known by the person who wrote it.

So how do the people in this illustration find out the true value of this mystery number? Simple: they find the person who wrote it and ask!

God's Word was written with the intent of making known the unknowable—of packaging the truth that He embodies in a way that we mortals can understand. Our search for spiritual and moral truth, therefore, will inevitably boil down to our search for God, and the answers have been found in the Bible all along.

God is truth. Make sure you're searching for Him, because He will be found.

 **FOR FURTHER THOUGHT:**

How is the statement "There is no truth" logically incoherent? How can a Christian man look past his culture's confusion to see the truth God provides?

> *God of truth, teach me never to settle for lies or to accept spiritual ignorance as a permanent condition. Keep drawing me further from my comfortable delusions and closer to Your reality.*

THE LIFE

Jesus said to him, "I am the way, the truth, and the life.
No man comes to the Father except through Me."
JOHN 14:6

Earlier, we discussed the fact that God is self-sufficient, which means He carries life permanently within Himself. "Life" is simply one of His necessary attributes.

But this is not exactly the same as the third attribute mentioned in John 14:6. Jesus is "life" in a sense that encompasses more than His own personal status; it extends also to those who believe in Him. In other words, He is life to us just as water and food and air are life to us and all the creatures on earth.

Without God, the inverse is true—only death awaits. Later, in John 15, Jesus expands upon this topic by saying, "I am the vine; you are the branches" (verse 5). Just as nutrients flow through the main vine to its many branches, thus keeping them alive, so Jesus serves as our conduit for spiritual life and strength. The moment one cuts off a branch, it withers and dies (verse 6). Similarly, the moment one begins rejecting Jesus is the moment spiritual death begins setting in. The nutrients still exist in the vine; they just no longer extend to the severed branch.

That's why it's so vital for a Christian man to "work out [his] own salvation with fear and trembling" (Philippians 2:12)—your relationship with God is simply too important to ignore.

 **FOR FURTHER THOUGHT:**

How are you maintaining your relationship with God? What are some obvious signs of a severed vine?

Lord Jesus, keep me connected to You. You're my vine—my life support—and I never want to cut myself off from Your presence.

I AM

And God said to Moses, "I Am That I Am."
And He said, "You shall say this to the children
of Israel, 'I Am has sent me to you.'"
Exodus 3:14

You'd be hard-pressed to find another Bible verse as chilling and awe-inspiring as this one. The words *I Am* carry with them such a sense of gravitas and mystery that even if this were the only verse in the Bible, you'd still be able to get a good picture of God's nature by reading it.

The first thing this attribute communicates to us is God's timeless status. Because He exists in the past, present, and future (more on that later in the book), there is no distinction to Him between what was and what will be. That's why the religious leaders of Jesus' day were so up in arms when Jesus said, "Before Abraham was, I am" (John 8:58). By stating things in such a grammatically unique way, Jesus was making clear His status as God—something the Jewish leaders didn't appreciate.

Which leads to the second aspect this statement to Moses reveals: God's mysteriousness. By breaking the rules of sentence structure, God was implicitly communicating His inherently indescribable status. The declaration "I Am

THAT I AM" is shorthand for, "I am so much more than anything you humans can imagine." And yet, by revealing Himself to Moses, God proved His willingness to connect with His creation.

Now, you have the opportunity to respond—to pursue a relationship with the timeless I AM.

 **FOR FURTHER THOUGHT:**

How does knowing that your future existence
is already known to God affect your life?
Do you feel glad or frustrated by the fact that
God's nature will never be fully comprehended?

*God of mysteries, whenever I come before You
I feel like an ant trying to comprehend the
universe. Teach me to approach Your truth
with a blend of curiosity and humility.*

WORTHY OF WORSHIP

*"Worthy is the Lamb who was slain to receive power and riches
and wisdom and strength and honor and glory and blessing."*
REVELATION 5:12

So far, we've looked at some of the ways we should respond
to each of God's singular attributes, but what about when we
combine them? How should we as Christians respond to the
embodiment of eternity, power, knowledge, love, justice, and
perfection?

We should worship Him.

Worshipping God is not just a good idea or a Sunday
morning exclusive. No, it's part of our moral obligation. God's
very nature demands that every other entity in existence fall
down before Him and worship Him as God. If we refuse, we
suffer the consequences.

So how does a Christian worship God? Through verbal
expression such as singing? Yes, that's part of it. But there
are so many other ways to worship Him. In fact, Romans
12:1 says, "Therefore I beseech you, brothers, by the mercies
of God, that you present your bodies as a living sacrifice, holy,
acceptable to God, which is your reasonable service." And
1 Corinthians 10:31 says, "Whatever you do, do all for the
glory of God."

So what exactly does worship look like? *Surrender*. It's complete surrender in every aspect of your life, even those areas that seem "secular" or unimportant. It's the purposeful subjection of your will to God's. It's the reason we should rise from bed each morning—the reason we exist.

God is worthy of our worship. Are you giving Him the honor He deserves?

 **FOR FURTHER THOUGHT:**

Why does this attribute of God fly in the face of our modern culture's values? How can a Christian man overcome his pride in order to worship the God who is worthy?

> *Lord, I will never be able to give You the endless praise You deserve—that's what heaven is for. Help me start today, however. I want my life to be a living song of worship for You.*

JEALOUS

"You shall worship no other god, for the LORD, whose name is Jealous, is a jealous God."

EXODUS 34:14

Today's verse is one that many Christians would like to conveniently sweep under the rug. After all, isn't jealousy a sin? Why would a holy God describe Himself using such a word? Was the Almighty actually just another tribal deity the Israelites worshipped?

No! While human jealousy is definitely a sin, it is perfectly right and natural for God. Why? Because as we've already seen, God owns (and deserves) everything. Therefore, His jealousy is really not jealousy at all—it's a claim to what is rightfully His.

Imagine saving money for years to buy a new car only for someone to steal it the next day. Would your desire to get your car back be wrong? Would anyone (other than the thief, perhaps) look at your situation and say, "Look how jealous he is"?

Of course not. You worked hard for that car, and it was rightfully yours. Similarly, all the praise we can offer God is already rightfully His—not because He worked for it but because He is perfect through and through. Therefore, when the Creator of the universe sees His children worshipping gods of wood, stone, and (in modern times) silicon, He has every right to chastise them for their theft of what exclusively belongs to Him.

God isn't cruel or unjust, but He does expect us to give Him what He deserves. The good news? Giving Him the praise He deserves will always be what's best for us too.

 FOR FURTHER THOUGHT:

Have you ever felt uncomfortable reading this verse? How can a better understanding of God's nature make verses like this one easier to swallow?

> *Lord, teach me to understand that Your jealousy is not petty or irrational. Give me the humility required to fall before You in praise.*

SELFLESS

"The Son of Man came not to be ministered to but to minister and to give His life as a ransom for many."
MATTHEW 20:28

As we learned yesterday, our God is jealous for our affections and devotion. This jealousy, however, is supplemented by another key attribute: His selflessness.

To understand how this works, start by remembering that because of God's righteousness and perfection, we have a moral obligation to be perfect in His sight and to worship Him exclusively. Failure to do so invites His judgment.

There's just one problem, though—none of us were able to live up to this impossibly high standard. So what did God do? Forsake His beloved image-bearers? Overlook their faults? Given God's perfect love and His perfect justice, neither option was acceptable to Him. Therefore, He took a third, more painful route, coming down to earth as one of us and selflessly taking on the punishment we deserve.

That's right: the second person of the Trinity—the Creator of the entire universe—willingly gave up His eternal, immortal glory to suffer the worst that this slimy, unfair, cruel world had to offer.

As Jesus said in John 15:13, "No man has greater love

than this, that a man lay down his life for his friends." Because God displayed His selflessness toward us, we should follow in His footsteps, being willing to lay down our own life for the good of our fellow man.

 FOR FURTHER THOUGHT:

How willing would you be to lay down your life for a stranger? What about for a friend? Are you laying down your life daily for God?

Selfless Lord, forgive me for the selfishness I have displayed in the past. Teach me to rise above my nature and to embrace your self-sacrificial love.

UNIQUE

"I am God, and there is no one like Me."
ISAIAH 46:9

According to the experts, the old adage "No two snowflakes are alike" is very likely true. Even though roughly a trillion trillion snowflakes fall to the ground each year, the atmospheric conditions that create them are so complex that it would be nearly impossible for them to churn out two identical flakes.

But to us, all snowflakes look the same. They may technically be unique, but practically they are identical. The same goes for pretty much everything that exists in our world. All things from rocks to plants to animals have their own quirks of design and structural differences, but also many similarities. Even when it comes to us humans, our variations and similarities are easily definable, so you can classify them and group them in ways that make sense.

Not so with God. He is unique in every sense of the word. When the Bible uses anthropomorphic language to describe Him, it does so because a fully accurate description of Him would be incomprehensible to us.

Once we fully comprehend that truth, it shouldn't be that hard to trust God, even when life seems chaotic and random. Why? Because in the midst of the loss and con-fusion, we are connected to the God who loves and knows us infinitely more than we can ever comprehend—and our unique God has everything under control.

 FOR FURTHER THOUGHT:

Do you sometimes think of God as merely an "improved" version of you? How can we grasp God's uniqueness while still cultivating a relationship with Him?

God, You are truly unique, while we are like snowflakes on Your hillside. Thank You for taking the time to be involved in each of our lives—caring for our every trivial concern.

BOUNDLESS

*Now to Him who is able to do exceedingly abundantly
above all that we ask or think, according to the
power that works in us, to Him be glory.*
Ephesians 3:20–21

When you pray for a need, do you have a habit of mentally setting limitations on God? In other words, do you pray only for the things you think God can do but leave out all the things you believe are just too impossible?

If so, the apostle Paul would like to have a word with you.

He was a man named Saul at first—a Christ-hating, Jewish extremist who actively worked to snuff out Christianity in its infancy. If you were a first-century Christian kneeling to pray for someone like that, how would your prayer go? "God, please put an obstacle in Saul's path. Or maybe make him lose interest so that he doesn't bother us anymore. Or maybe just send down a convenient lightning bolt or something."

No doubt, a lot of such prayers ascended to heaven in those days. But how many do you think included the words, "Lord, make Saul a missionary for You"?

We will never know—but we do know that if there was someone out there praying that prayer, God answered it to perfection. Not only did God change the trajectory of Saul's life, He changed his heart, motivating him to spread the good news of Jesus to as many cultures as he could, as well as to write a hefty portion of scripture itself.

Are you recognizing God's boundless power when you pray?

 FOR FURTHER THOUGHT:

Are there any prayers that God does not want us to pray? If so, what might these be? How has your prayer life been affected by what you've learned about God's character?

> *Boundless Lord, expand my understanding of Your power. I never want to place limits on You with my prayers.*

LORD

*If you confess with your mouth the Lord Jesus
and believe in your heart that God has raised
Him from the dead, you shall be saved.*

ROMANS 10:9

Today's verse might be confusing for those who remember James 2:19, which says, "You believe that there is one God. You do well; the demons also believe, and tremble." That verse, coupled with a few occasions in which demons not only believed but confessed Jesus' status as the Son of God (Mark 1:23–24, 3:11; Luke 4:41), may be enough to make a devout Christian feel uneasy. After all, if demons fulfill both requirements of today's passage and yet are obviously not saved from punishment, who is to say that *we* are any different?

The answer lies in one easily overlooked word in today's verse: *Lord.*

Lord isn't merely a title that uniquely applies to Jesus— it's a word that carries with it the idea of an authoritative relationship with other beings, similar to the word *master.* So by confessing Jesus as Lord, a person is not just intellectually agreeing with a fact; rather, that person is implicitly admitting—and submitting to—Jesus' authority.

In other words, this confession is actually a pledge of loyalty.

Of course, Jesus is Lord whether or not you acknowledge that He is. But the moment you confess Him as such, you begin your journey toward an everlasting life with Him as Your eternal Master.

 FOR FURTHER THOUGHT:

Are demons capable of confessing Jesus as Lord? Why or why not? Does your faith go beyond belief to include submission?

Lord, I believe You exist and that You loved me enough to die in my place. I surrender my life— my wants, passions, and dreams—to You. Use me.

THE BEGINNING

*"I am Alpha and Omega, the beginning and
the ending," says the Lord, "who is, and who
was, and who is to come, the Almighty."*

REVELATION 1:8

"In the beginning was the Word, and the Word was with God, and the Word was God."

These are the opening words of the Gospel of John—the same John who recorded Jesus' words in the book of Revelation. But today's verse expands on John 1:1 by emphasizing that Jesus wasn't just there at the beginning, He *was* the beginning.

Alpha is the first letter in the Greek alphabet, so Jesus' use of that term implied that everything that exists began with Him—He is the "uncaused cause" of all things, the one who kick-started this cosmic drama.

This is hard for us to grasp, yet simple logic points to this great truth. After all, it's obvious that any string of events must have a first event—the chain can't go back forever! Well, Jesus is that first event. He is the beginning. He is the Alpha.

What this means for us is that there is really no such thing as a self-made man. Sure, you may have put a lot of effort into getting where you are today, but all the resources you used along the way—even the motivation that drove you forward—were provided by Jesus, who both made you and knew your every action long before the world began.

Once we recognize Jesus as our beginning, it becomes so much easier to make Him our middle and our end as well.

 **FOR FURTHER THOUGHT:**

Do you sometimes take credit for the blessings in your life? How can we learn to recognize Jesus—not ourselves—as the source of every good thing?

Lord Jesus, forgive me for all the times I have seen myself as the cause of my good fortune. Open my eyes to the fact that You have always been here, bringing me to where I am today.

THE END

*"I am Alpha and Omega, the beginning and
the ending," says the Lord, "who is, and who
was, and who is to come, the Almighty."*

Many a Hollywood production has been built around this one question: When the end comes, who will survive? The ones trained in self-defense? Doomsday preppers who have fifteen hundred jars of peanut butter in the cellar? The really lucky ones?

The true answer might seem a little less satisfying—no one will. Second Peter 3:12 speaks of "the coming of the day of God, in which the heavens being on fire shall be dissolved and the elements shall melt with fervent heat." If you're still around when that happens, all your prepping and training will be useless. Today's verse implies that Jesus alone will withstand the end of all things. Even more, He will be the cause of it. He will *be* the end.

But don't fret! First Corinthians 15:51–52 says that all the believers who are still alive at that time won't have to face the end at all. Rather, we'll all be "changed, in a moment, in the twinkling of an eye, at the last trumpet." Our bodies won't burn with the elements—we'll be given new bodies and transported to be with Jesus as this worn-down universe dissolves (1 Thessalonians 4:17).

Sure, surviving the apocalypse might make for an exciting story, but Jesus offers us a real-life fire escape plan. In a world that seems worse by the day, take courage in knowing the ending—and the end, Jesus Himself.

🔆 FOR FURTHER THOUGHT:

How does knowing that everything you see will one day dissolve change your perspective? How can a Christian man learn to avoid placing too much stock in this life?

Lord, I look forward to the day when I can see You face to face forever. For now, keep my priorities straight so that when that day comes, I'll be ready for the sudden transformation.

THE MIDDLE

"I am Alpha and Omega, the beginning and the ending," says the Lord, "who is, and who was, and who is to come, the Almighty."

<small>REVELATION 1:8</small>

When thinking about Jesus' status in relation to time, we often dwell on the first half of today's verse, seeing only the beginning and end. It's easier that way. We can all visualize Jesus creating the universe, and it's not hard to think of Him ending it someday in the future. But what about right now? What about the Jesus who *is*—the one who exists alongside us in this messy world today?

It can be hard to reconcile the imperfection we see today with the knowledge that our perfect God is still at work in it all. But it's true. And would you like to guess what God's primary instrument is when it comes to His present-day work? Luke 17:20–21 provides the answer—"The kingdom of God does not come with observation, nor shall they say, 'Look here!' or 'Look there!' For behold, the kingdom of God is within you."

That's right—God's main tool in today's world is the church. And this isn't some vague generalization—since you are (hopefully) a part of God's church, Jesus' words apply directly to you.

First Corinthians 6:19 says "your body is the temple of the Holy Spirit," meaning the God of today is dwelling within you now, eager to use your talents to change this sin-stricken world. All you have to do is let Him take control.

🔅 FOR FURTHER THOUGHT:

In what ways can a Christian offer God total control of his life? How can dwelling on God's active role in today's world increase our sense of urgency?

> *Lord, thank You for not abandoning us to the shifting winds of today. Use me at this moment in whatever way You please. I am Your vessel—from now until the end.*

INFINITE

"Will God indeed dwell on the earth? Behold, the heavens and heaven of heavens cannot contain You."
1 Kings 8:27

The cosmos is a big place. According to our best estimates, the observable universe (the part of it we can see) is so huge that it would take a beam of light ninety-three billion years to travel all the way across. Not only that, space itself is expanding at a tremendous rate, and there may be a near-infinite amount of it that lies beyond our view.

But today's verse says that not even this vast, inky ocean can contain God, the one who made it all.

Why? Because God is infinite. All language pertaining to size and power breaks down when we discuss our infinite God. He has no size—He simply *is*, everywhere and beyond (as we've already seen earlier in this book). His power does not have an upper limit. His past and future bleed together into an eternal present. His love is unending.

As finite beings, we can become confused or frustrated when we hear such descriptions. We often crave a God we can understand, so we make our own, fashioning tiny, petty idols whose every wish and whim mysteriously aligns with ours. All the while the infinite God patiently waits, watching as we grow bored with our manmade deities. And then, when we finally realize the absurdity of the life we've been chasing, He welcomes us not with anger but with lovingly open arms.

Surrender yourself to the infinite God. You'll find He's exactly the right size for you.

 FOR FURTHER THOUGHT:

Why is it impossible for God to be fully understood?
Does dwelling on the idea of God's infinity
make you uneasy, or does it offer comfort?

Infinite God, thank You for involving Yourself in the affairs of us finite beings. I want to pursue You as my source of meaning, not these temporal pleasures I see all around.

RIGHTEOUS

*Righteous You are, O LORD,
and upright are Your judgments.*
PSALM 119:137

It's common in movies and television shows for ministers and devout Christians to be depicted as corrupt hypocrites, preaching righteousness while practicing hate and selfishness.

Given the existence of many real-life believers who resemble their fictional caricatures, it's not hard to see why the church has fallen out of favor in the eyes of unbelievers. How many seemingly upright preachers have plummeted from grace through the shocking revelation of some hidden scandal? How many Christians—maybe even ones you know—harbor skeletons in their closet that, if revealed, would cast doubt on their devotion? And how many times have we ourselves scolded someone for his behavior, only to realize we've been guilty of that same sin?

For fallen humans, the disconnect between our words and our actions is a somber reality. Today's verse, however, says that God's righteousness is different. It isn't just for show. It is as real as He Himself is. In fact, God is inseparable from His righteousness. If God behaved unrighteously even for a moment, He would, by definition, be disqualified from being the one, true God.

For God, no disconnect exists. His words match His actions, 100 percent.

So don't put your trust in a preacher or an organization or even in the church itself. Place all your trust in the God who will never cease to be righteous.

 **FOR FURTHER THOUGHT:**

Have you ever been let down by the church? How can a Christian be active in the church while keeping his faith exclusively in the church's head—Jesus?

Righteous God, thank You for being righteous when I am not. Help me to learn from Your consistent moral perfection.

PERSONAL

Our God is in the heavens;
He has done whatever He has pleased.
PSALM 115:3

Our culture is enamored with the idea of an impersonal God—a being that governs all reality but doesn't really have a will of His own. A force of nature, perhaps, that ties everything together but is ultimately impossible to know in any meaningful way. An emotion. A vibe. Karma. Fate.

All these descriptions (some more insightful than others) leave out one truth: our God is a personal God, not some pantheistic energy or cold natural law.

Genesis 1:27 says God used His own image as a blueprint for the creation of humanity. We're living souls not because of some emergent property in our brains but because God Himself is a living soul, complete with all the attributes that normally come to mind when we think of a sentient being. Free will, the capacity for love and compassion, emotion, desire—all these attributes belong to God, albeit in a perfect way.

Attributing our blessings to fate or the will of the universe isn't just meaningless but a slap in the face to the God who actively chose to grant us the benefits we enjoy. And putting our faith in karma to save us is equally egregious. Our salvation comes from the God who willingly chose to enter His creation and die so that we could obtain the life we don't deserve.

Why settle for some hollow, New Age worldview when you can serve the personal God who loves you?

 FOR FURTHER THOUGHT:

Do you sometimes think of God as an impersonal entity? Why or why not? How can understanding God's personal nature affect the way you pray, worship, and live?

Personal God, thank You for being more than an impersonal Creator. I want to know You better, so motivate me to spend more time in Your Word today.

LIGHT

God is light and in Him is no darkness at all.
1 JOHN 1:5

The classical thinker Plato once gave an illustration involving a group of people who have spent their lives chained up inside a cave, their backs facing the entrance. For years, this group watched the elegant play of shadows on the cavern walls, unable to imagine any reality greater.

One day someone stumbles in and, seeing one of the cave dwellers, mercifully frees him from his chains. The former cave dweller walks outside and is immediately blinded by the sun's light—something he'd never witnessed until that day. The light scares him, but it also fascinates him.

Eventually he works up the courage to open his eyes and let the light in, gradually becoming more accustomed to the amazing sights now exploding in his vision. Ecstatic, he rushes back into the cave in an effort to convince his fellow prisoners that there is a whole new world just outside the cave entrance that they must see. His friends, however, are convinced that his eyesight has been ruined by exposure to something outside the cave and that it is they who are correctly perceiving reality. They refuse to leave the cave and the "comfort" they have enjoyed.

We were all cave dwellers once. God is light, and the moment you decided to let His light into your life, darkness just didn't hold the same appeal. Some people will see you and want a taste of your freedom; others will push back in fear of what they don't understand.

But no matter how rejected you feel, never stop pointing others to the light. An exodus from the cave may be just around the corner.

 **FOR FURTHER THOUGHT:**

What similarities does God share with light?
How has He illuminated your life?

> *Lord of light, thank You for pulling me from the darkness I once enjoyed. May I never give up in my quest to shine Your light to those still living in the cave of sin.*

SLOW TO ANGER

The LORD is merciful and gracious,
slow to anger and abundant in mercy.
PSALM 103:8

Ephesians 4:26 says, "Be angry and do not sin." This command may seem hard to follow, but here's some good news: most of us guys have the first half down already!

Okay, maybe we're being a bit too sarcastic. But isn't it true? When someone cuts us off—whether in traffic or in conversation—how eager are we to push the ANGER button and let our worst impulses take control? No matter how civilized we may think ourselves, the moment someone steals our parking place that deep, dark part of the back of our brains lights up, and we're suddenly back in 3000 BC, ready to dish out some pain with a club.

Today's verse says that, unlike humans, God is *slow* to anger. Whereas anger is often our default emotion, God's default emotion is love, and it takes a consistently arrogant, unrepentant person to make Him truly angry.

In other words, the popular concept of God as some old, embittered man with a lightning bolt in his hand is the stuff of comic strips, not good, biblical theology. A false god like Zeus might fit that description, but our God is head and shoulders above any petty deity mankind can dream up.

Love, not pain, is God's weapon of choice. And since we're called to imitate God, each of us should strive to make our anger reaction time more in line with His.

 FOR FURTHER THOUGHT:

In what ways are you striving to reduce your anger reaction time? How can studying Jesus' life and teachings make a Christian more willing to be gentle?

Lord, thank You for being much slower to anger than I am. Teach me to adopt Your mercy as my default behavior when dealing with others.

WONDERFUL

*A Child is born to us, a Son is given to us, and the
government shall be on His shoulder. And His name
shall be called Wonderful, Counselor, the Mighty God,
the Everlasting Father, the Prince of Peace.*
Isaiah 9:6

Today's verse says that one of Jesus' many titles is *Wonderful*, implying His birth would be more than just an interesting footnote of history. When a person discovers something wonderful, it doesn't just generate dinner table conversation. It radically changes one's life and worldview, giving that individual a burning desire to share this discovery with others.

The Greek mathematician Archimedes, according to popular legend, was once charged with proving that a crown made for the king was really composed of solid gold. As he pondered how to measure the crown's mass, Archimedes decided to take a refreshing bath. Slipping into the tub, he noticed his own body's mass was displacing the water, thus giving him an idea for the perfect way to calculate the mass of any object. Thrilled, Archimedes leaped out of his tub and ran out onto the streets unclothed, yelling, "*Eureka!*"—Greek for "I found it!" as he rushed to bring word to the king.

Archimedes found something wonderful that day, and his

excitement was uncontainable. Similarly, we should be enthusiastic beyond words about Jesus, willing to proclaim His good news no matter what others might think.

We Christians have made a wonderful discovery. How can we but help from hitting the streets?

 **FOR FURTHER THOUGHT:**

In what ways are you proclaiming your wonderful Savior? What should our response be when others fail to see the wonder in our message?

Wonderful Lord, thank You for infusing my life with a sense of exciting purpose and fulfillment. I never want to lose this spark of unbridled joy.

COUNSELOR

His name shall be called. . .Counselor.

Continuing with the list of attributes found in Isaiah 9:6, we see that Jesus is described as "Counselor."

But what kind of counselor is He? After all, a plethora of counselors exists. Some aim at improving one's business practices while others claim to strengthen a person's inner well-being. But with our Lord, the counsel is all-encompassing.

Need financial counseling? Jesus said in Matthew 22:21, "Render to Caesar the things that are Caesar's and to God the things that are God's." God's Word also instructs, "Owe no man anything but to love one another" (Romans 13:8).

What about personal counseling? Ecclesiastes says that your purpose is found in this one command: "Fear God and keep His commandments" (12:13), so no existential crisis on our part is necessary. And if you're struggling with fear, 1 Peter 5:7 says to cast "all your care on [God], for He cares for you."

But what if your marriage is falling apart and you need some heavy-duty counseling? Ephesians 5:25 says, "Husbands, love your wives, even as Christ also loved the church and gave Himself for it." After all, you can't go wrong with learning the art of self-sacrificial love from the one who perfected it.

And if you need spiritual counseling, well, your divine expert oversaw a collection of sixty-six books on that topic alone. You might want to check it out!

 FOR FURTHER THOUGHT:

Do you go to God and His Word for wise counsel? When should a Chrisitan listen to or ignore the counsel given by others?

Lord, Your wisdom makes You the perfect counselor for me. Teach me to make use of Your guidance each day.

PRINCE OF PEACE

His name shall be called. . .the Prince of Peace.
ISAIAH 9:6

The last attribute mentioned in today's passage is "Prince of Peace."

But what if your life isn't peaceful? What if you can't pay your bills, and each grocery run hurts way more than it should? What if your wife or child or best friend is in a coma in the hospital, and the doctors aren't sure what to do? What if you've just been diagnosed with an incurable disease?

Where's the peace in that?

Jesus said in John 14:27, "I leave peace with you; I give to you My peace. I do not give to you as the world gives." The world's peace is merely a shallow comfort—a feeling without a foothold in reality. It offers no consolation that your life has meaning; rather, it serves only to make you feel cozy right now, lulling you into a sense of false security. This isn't peace. It's deception.

Jesus' peace is achieved only by learning the truth, not by telling yourself a lie. It confirms that your life *does* have purpose and that there *is* a greater reward ahead, making whatever trials you face now seem trivial in comparison to the joy you know is coming.

Jesus is the Prince of Peace, and any "peace" found outside His domain will only lead to chaos. Which peace are you pursuing?

 **FOR FURTHER THOUGHT:**

Have you ever sought peace apart from Jesus? How did that turn out? Why is it so easy sometimes for us to forsake our only true peace in favor of a counterfeit?

Prince of Peace, You are my order in the midst of chaos. Teach me to find my contentment and happiness solely in You.

FAITHFUL

And I saw heaven opened, and behold, a white horse.
And He who sat on him was called Faithful and True,
and in righteousness He judges and makes war.
REVELATION 19:11

In 1870, members of the Washburn expedition stumbled upon an astonishing sight: a scalding fountain that periodically erupted from the earth, reaching heights of nearly two hundred feet at times. Impressed by the geyser's regularity, they dubbed the fountain "Old Faithful"—a name that's stuck ever since.

What you might not know, however, is that Old Faithful isn't as faithful as its name suggests. Its eruption intervals can range from 35 minutes to 120. In fact, since its discovery in 1870, its average wait time has noticeably lengthened. This, along with the fact that its eruptions don't always reach maximum height, has led to disappointment in tourists expecting a truly "faithful" performance.

But unlike this Yellowstone geyser, God earns His title "Faithful." When people come to Him for salvation and spiritual healing, He doesn't disappoint them with a less-than-impressive showing. No, He always comes through, and His gifts always exceed the petitioner's expectations.

Pleas for forgiveness are granted with the guarantee of an eternal life with Him. Prayers for healing are granted with better health now or simply the promise of a future existence without pain. Requests for comfort are granted with a renewed sense of purpose and a fundamental change in outlook.

Old Faithful may or may not be worth the gasoline it takes to get there. But the price for meeting the true "Faithful" is entirely free. . .and it will always be worth your time.

 FOR FURTHER THOUGHT:

How has God been faithful in your life?
Is His faithfulness always immediately apparent,
or does it sometimes take time to be seen more fully?

*Faithful God, thank You for showing up whenever
Your children call on You. Teach me to recognize
Your faithfulness wherever it may appear.*

PHYSICIAN

When Jesus heard it, He said to them, "Those who are
well have no need of the physician, but those who are sick.
I came to call not the righteous but sinners to repentance."
MARK 2:17

Shuntaro Hida was six kilometers from Hiroshima when the
bomb dropped. Rushing outside to see what had caused the
blinding flash, Hida was thrown off his feet by the ensuing
shockwave. Horrified, he watched the distant mushroom
cloud expand into the blue sky, glowing an unearthly yellow.
Panic soon gave way to resolve, however, as Hida jumped onto
his bike and pedaled into the city, searching for survivors.

What he found was beyond horrific: thousands of bloody
civilians roamed the streets, their bodies torn and bleeding.
But Hida had been trained for this. One by one, he began
treating the injured—and as the effects of radiation sickness
started to manifest themselves in the following days, he began
treating that too, launching him into a lifelong journey dedi-
cated to better understanding and curing this ghastly disease.

When sin exploded onto the scene in the garden of Eden,
its toxins spread throughout all humanity, leaving us all spiritually torn. Jesus, however, didn't turn His face from the car-
nage. Instead, He took action, coming to our place with a

singular goal: to cure us all of this terrible sickness. But unlike an earthly physician, Jesus never has an upper limit on the number of patients He can treat. All who need healing can receive it immediately—just for the asking.

 ## FOR FURTHER THOUGHT:

What are some of the specific sicknesses Jesus has healed you of? Are you ever hesitant to ask Him for the treatment you need? Why or why not?

> *Healing Lord, You alone hold the power to heal disease—physical and spiritual. Teach me to trust You as my great physician.*

ANCIENT OF DAYS

"I watched until the thrones were put down, and the Ancient of Days, whose garment was white as snow, and the hair of His head like pure wool, sat. His throne was like a fiery flame, and His wheels like burning fire."

DANIEL 7:9

Age inspires awe.

When we look at an ancient oak tree with thousands of straggling limbs, we begin to imagine all the storms this behemoth has endured. When we look at the sturdy mountains, thoughts may pass through our minds about the countless years and shifting geological events that have refined them into their present appearance. And when scientists discover fossils of long-extinct creatures, we might marvel at the ages through which these priceless relics have lain hidden in the dirt.

God, however, predates them all.

He is, as Daniel describes Him in today's passage, the Ancient of Days—the unchanging monolith who has existed throughout eternity past and who will continue through eternity future. There isn't a number in all of mathematics that could communicate His age, for He is ageless. Without beginning and without end, He is the very foundation of time itself.

When we think of God, we should remember we are mere mortals contemplating the eternal. All pride should give way to awe. Praise should be the gasp that escapes our lips. Worship should be our state of mind.

God is the Ancient of Days. Yet He has given you the opportunity to know Him right now. That is the most awe-inspiring truth of them all.

 **FOR FURTHER THOUGHT:**

When you think of God's eternality, does your life start seeming all too short? How can a Christian be at peace with this life's brevity?

> *God, out of all the events that have transpired throughout history—all the events You have watched and overseen—You still choose to intervene in my life. Thank You for Your timeless love.*

CARING

Casting all your care on Him, for He cares for you.
1 PETER 5:7

Imagine walking through the woods one day and finding an anthill. Thousands of busy insects march in tiny, black rivulets that flow smoothly through the dirt. Some seem to defy gravity, hauling massive crumbs up to the summit before plunging into its pinpoint crater. Others branch out from the pack, their nearly microscopic antennae eagerly twitching in response to stimuli known only to them.

How likely are you to be concerned for the plight of this tiny civilization? A rainstorm may come tonight and wash all of these hapless creatures away. Do you care? Many of these ants may come back to their anthill hungry—a few might even starve. Will you lose a second of sleep thinking about their well-being?

Probably not. These ants are so far removed from us in size and intelligence that we simply act as if they don't exist.

Aren't you glad God sees us differently? To Him, we're even smaller than ants, each of us crawling on this tiny anthill called Earth. Still, God cares about our plight. Even more, He wants to enter our lives and form deeper relationships with us than we could ever form among ourselves.

When seen in this light, God's care for us may seem irrational. But God has never been concerned about conforming to our standards of "normal." He simply keeps caring for us, even when we give Him every reason not to do so.

God definitely cares for you. How well are you reciprocating?

 FOR FURTHER THOUGHT:

Do you ever feel forgotten by God? During those times, how might you gain a better understanding of how much He cares?

Lord, You care about my life even more than I do.
When I'm tempted to make destructive choices,
You redirect me down a better path. Thank You.

COMPASSIONATE

Jesus went forth and saw a great multitude and was moved with compassion for them, and He healed their sick.
MATTHEW 14:14

Saying you care for someone and showing compassion toward that person are two entirely different things. One involves a mental state—the acknowledgement that a person's well-being affects your emotions to some degree. The other involves acting on these emotions to the point that you step in to intervene.

In today's passage, Jesus did more than simply care for the multitudes; He had compassion on them. He didn't just look on them with pity and say, "Be warmed and filled," then send them on their way (James 2:16). No, He saw their suffering, and their suffering prompted Him to act. As a result, many walked away healed that day, never to be the same again.

What are we to do with God's compassion? First and most obviously, we should accept it. This means receiving the remedy to our helpless predicament of sin—Jesus' sacrifice. Next, we should actively thank Him for the blessings that continually flow from His compassion. And finally, we should strive to follow His compassionate example in our dealings with others. Experience, after all, is the best teacher, so a person who feels God's compassion through you is much more likely to accept the Lord than someone who sees only selfishness in the church.

No man is too tough for compassion, especially the love and mercy that God offers. Be sure you open your heart and mind to His kindness, today and every day.

 **FOR FURTHER THOUGHT:**

Is compassion ever convenient? How is selflessness necessary for showing compassion?

> *God, teach me to react to others' needs with compassion instead of annoyance or apathy. You showed compassion toward me when I didn't deserve it. Help me do the same for others.*

EMPATHETIC

We do not have a high priest who cannot be concerned
with the feeling of our weaknesses, but was in all
points tempted as we are, yet without sin.
HEBREWS 4:15

If care is admirable and compassion even more so, then empathy is the final step toward the perfect love God possesses. Empathy means not just pitying someone but actively experiencing that person's plight as if it were your own.

Have you ever seen someone get hurt in a way you've experienced before, and just the sight of it caused your pain receptors to fire? If so, you've experienced a small taste of the empathy God feels toward us. When Jesus came to earth, He braved a life full of rejection (John 1:11), hunger (Matthew 4:2), homelessness (Matthew 8:20), sadness to the point of weeping (John 11:35), betrayal (Matthew 26:47–49), and even agonizing dread (Luke 22:44). And then at His passion and crucifixion, He experienced suffering that few can even imagine—let alone relate to.

In short, every negative experience that is humanly possible for us to experience—even temptation, as seen in today's verse—has already been experienced by Jesus.

What a comfort! To know that you are not alone in your

suffering makes all the difference. And when you face the devastatingly powerful allure of temptation, you can stand strong, knowing Jesus—who faced this enemy and won—is empathizing with you and empowering your will to resist.

 FOR FURTHER THOUGHT:

How strongly are you able to empathize with another person's pain? How does it feel to know that Jesus has experienced the disappointment and sadness you feel today?

Lord, thank You for being an empathetic God. No matter how hard life gets, You are always there to share my pains and burdens.

INVISIBLE

*[Jesus] is the image of the invisible God,
the firstborn of every creature.*
COLOSSIANS 1:15

God has gifted us with five wonderful senses, each designed for detecting unique aspects of the world we inhabit. But as amazing as these senses are, they are not exhaustive in their capabilities. There will always be things that lie beyond their range. The law of gravity, for instance, is just as real as this book you're reading, but you can't see, hear, touch, taste, or smell it. It can only be "seen" as numbers and equations on a page—symbols that point to an invisible force.

Similarly, God Himself exceeds the ability of our senses to comprehend Him. Even more, He exists in a realm outside our three-dimensional universe, so any instruments we devise will never be able to detect His presence. But just as it's silly to deny the law of gravity because it can't be seen, it's equally foolish to reject God's existence simply because He cannot be confined to a petri dish in a lab.

As well-intentioned as some Christians might be, it is ultimately a fruitless endeavor to attempt to scientifically "prove" God's existence. Trying to detect His presence with microscopes and test tubes will be about as productive as trying to measure the mass of the sun with a bathroom scale.

Rather, since God is a Spirit (as we have already learned), we find Him through the means He has provided—by reading His Word, praying, and meditating on His truth.

Only when we realize this can we learn to see beyond our eyesight.

 **FOR FURTHER THOUGHT:**

Why do you think God stays "hidden"? If he would reveal Himself physically, do you think more people would be saved? (For additional thought: How did that go for the Israelites?)

Invisible God, I don't need to see You to know You exist—I feel You living in me each day. May others see just how real You are.

CLEARLY SEEN

*From the creation of the world the invisible things
of Him are clearly seen, being understood by the
things that are made, even His eternal power and
Godhead, so that they are without excuse.*

ROMANS 1:20

Yesterday, we used the illustration of the law of gravity to speak of God's invisible nature. But you could take this comparison one step further. Just as the invisible law of gravity is "clearly seen" throughout creation (by way of the earth's orbit and our ability to walk on the planet's surface, among other evidences), so God's presence is "clearly seen" all around us (in our sense of morality, the beauty that fills the universe, and many other ways).

In John 3:8, Jesus gives an even more evocative illustration: "The wind blows where it wishes, and you hear the sound of it but cannot tell where it comes from and where it goes. So is everyone who is born of the Spirit." In other words, just as the shaking of the trees in a thunderstorm signals the arrival of a powerful but invisible wind, so the transformation that occurs within a believer's heart signifies the arrival of our all-powerful God.

God has invaded our reality, filling it so thoroughly with

signs of His presence that it would take a fool to miss all the clues (see Psalm 14:1). As a result, anyone who ignores God and tries to live apart from His laws will stand condemned, "without excuse" on Judgment Day.

God may be invisible, but His presence is unmistakable. All you have to do is look.

 **FOR FURTHER THOUGHT:**

In what areas is God's presence most obvious to you? Why do so many people go out of their way to ignore or explain away these obvious clues?

Father, may each sunset I see remind me of You, and may You make Yourself even more amazingly known through the work You do in my heart.

GENEROUS

If any of you lacks wisdom, let him ask of God,
who gives to all men generously and without
reproach, and it shall be given him.

JAMES 1:5

You've probably heard the expression, "Give till it hurts." Perhaps you've even tried to live by this motto when it came time for Christmas shopping and Sunday morning offerings. What you may not realize, however, is that God Himself is so generous that He too "gave till it hurt."

Jesus was under no obligation to give His life for our sins—He could have let us rot in our misdeeds and unrighteousness. But because He is love personified, He gave up everything. But Jesus' death was not the only way He proved His generosity. Throughout His time on earth, the Son of God committed to an attitude of servanthood, seeking the well-being of the masses over Himself. In all of His interactions with people, others came first in Jesus' mind.

This type of generosity went so much further than plinking a few coins into the synagogue plate—it was a radical outlook that influenced His behavior in life and in death. And now, seated at the Father's right hand, Jesus is *still* exercising generosity, interceding for His children (Romans 8:34).

Though God has an infinite supply of everything—wisdom, power, you name it—He still found a way to "give till it hurts." Are you that zealous in your generosity?

 **FOR FURTHER THOUGHT:**

Do you sometimes see God as reluctant to grant your requests? Does God's generosity guarantee He will always answer our prayers the way we would like?

Generous Lord, thank You for assuring me that there is not a request too bold to bring before You. Help me to discern Your will for me when I come before You.

A CONSUMING FIRE

"The LORD your God is a consuming fire."
DEUTERONOMY 4:24

Ever heard of Icarus? He was the young man in Greek mythology whose father gave him a pair of wings made from feathers, threads and, fatefully, beeswax. These wings could carry him out of the prison he was in, but he was not to fly too close to the sun.

You can probably guess what happened next: he flew too close to the sun. Instantly, his wings began to melt mid-flight, sending Icarus tumbling fatally into the sea.

Today, we know that the sun is far hotter than the ancients could have ever guessed. The surface of this life-giving ball of energy stays at a balmy ten thousand degrees Fahrenheit, while its core reaches temperatures of twenty-seven million! The sun is necessary for life to exist on our planet, but get too close and the sun's immense heat becomes deadly.

For the ancient Israelites, God was their sun (see Malachi 4:2). He created them and sustained them, but His holiness was simply too great for them to get too close. They had to observe His splendor from afar lest they meet a fate worse than that of Icarus. God was a consuming fire for anyone who dared approach Him or transgress His commands.

Thankfully, Jesus' sacrifice has changed things for us. Our God is still a consuming fire (Hebrews 12:29), but only for those who refuse to follow Him. For those of us sanctified by Jesus' blood, who have received His holiness in place of our own, we can "come boldly" before God in prayer (Hebrews 4:16), unafraid to accidentally fly too close to the sun.

 ## FOR FURTHER THOUGHT:

Are you sometimes afraid of approaching God in prayer? Is it ever possible for a Christian to get too close to God?

> *Lord, though I revere You as a consuming fire, I also understand that Jesus' work on the cross prevents me from being consumed. Thank You for the opportunity to draw closer to You.*

WARRIOR

The LORD is a man of war. The LORD is His name.
EXODUS 15:3

It was July of 1794, and a group of about five hundred agitated insurrectionists had gathered near Pittsburgh to oppose a tax on distillery products. As the protests quickly snowballed into threats of violence, George Washington soon realized drastic measures would have to be taken. If not, his fledgling nation would plunge into anarchy before the wheels of democracy could ever start turning.

Therefore, the president authorized a full-scale military response to this insurgency and, on September 30 of the same year, mounted his horse to lead his thirteen thousand troops against the rebels. Thankfully, violence was averted when the insurrectionists dispersed before troops arrived, preserving the American experiment.

As some have noted, this remains the only time in history that a sitting American president ever led troops into battle. But as Christians, we serve a leader who is no stranger to riding into battle alongside us. God is never afraid to muddy His boots for the good of His children. He even went so far as to become a human being and live in this grimy world for three decades, just so we'd have a chance to live with Him in glory forever.

Just as those troops in 1794, seeing their president riding triumphantly just ahead of them, must have received a morale boost for the ages, so we can ride fearlessly into spiritual battle each day, trusting our warrior God to give us the victory.

 FOR FURTHER THOUGHT:

How can a man know if he is on God's winning side?
What are some instances in scripture where God
stood strong with the nation of Israel in battle?

Lord Jesus, thank You for getting Your hands dirty on my behalf—for suffering the pain of crucifixion when I was the one who deserved to die. Remind me always of Your strengthening presence.

VICTORIOUS

Thanks be to God, who gives us the victory through our Lord Jesus Christ.
1 CORINTHIANS 15:57

It's great to know your leader is a warrior who fights alongside you in battle. But a warrior's presence is only as comforting as his likelihood of winning. In other words, if you were following a leader with a reputation as a poor commander, you would probably not feel as enthusiastic if you saw him riding before you.

That's why it's so important for the Christian to have a proper understanding of God's nature. Since He is omnipotent (as discussed earlier) that means, by definition, He *cannot lose.* The moment you join God's side is the moment you win. It's as simple as that. It's an automatic victory for the persevering child of God. Even though you'll never win a battle in your life, God will win them for you.

Jesus Himself has taken on the devil and emerged unscathed, holding the keys of hell (Revelation 1:18). He looked crucifixion squarely in the eye then walked away, dragging death by its hair and throwing it into the tomb forever (1 Corinthians 15:54–55). His Word has endured the hatred and vitriol of a billion blasphemous tongues, but it always comes out on top (Matthew 24:35).

There's never been a battle God has lost, nor will there ever be. So today, no matter how strong the army of trials and doubts may seem, you can rest assured: Jesus is winning your war.

 FOR FURTHER THOUGHT:

Do you sometimes struggle to believe
that God will be victorious? How can you
strengthen your faith in His ability to win?

*God, when all the battles of history are over and
the universe as we know it ends, You will stand
as the ultimate victor. Teach me to trust Your
victory and to always stay on Your side.*

FORGIVING

You, being dead in your sins and the uncircumcision
of your flesh, He has made alive together with
Him, having forgiven you all trespasses.
Colossians 2:13

Imagine getting a phone call, and the voice on the other end tells you the worst news imaginable: your only son has been shot and killed at school. You rush to the scene to find the perpetrator, a young man, still soaked in blood, on his knees pleading for your forgiveness.

In that moment, very few would hold you accountable for your actions. But imagine that instead of giving this man the lashing he deserves, you grant his request. Seeing the genuine sorrow in his eyes, you lift him to his feet and embrace him. Then, in the following weeks, you meet regularly with this man in prison, developing a friendship with him and refusing to bring up his horrific crime. And finally, realizing that this man has no family of his own, you adopt him as your own son.

This unthinkable series of events is exactly what God has done for us. We were all complicit in the death of His only Son, Jesus—in fact, our sins are the very thing that nailed Him to the cross. We're all guilty of deicide, of murdering the divine. Yet in response to our unthinkable crime, God has done something equally unthinkable: He has forgiven us and adopted us as His children.

Today, thank God for His radical forgiveness.

 **FOR FURTHER THOUGHT:**

Is it possible for us to forgive the way God has forgiven us? Why or why not? In what way does a proper understanding of God's forgiveness motivate us not to sin?

God, thank You for giving me the one thing I deserve the least: Your forgiveness. Teach me to show Your great forgiveness when others wrong me in far lesser ways.

REFUGE

*I cried to You, O LORD. I said, "You are my refuge
and my portion in the land of the living."*
PSALM 142:5

There's an old joke that goes something like this: "Question: How'd the guy who drank poison in his house keep from dying? Answer: He was standing in the living room."

The reason this joke is funny (or sad, depending on your sense of humor) is due to its absurdity. Your living room is no more likely to save you from death than your kitchen or bathroom—it's just a pun on the name. In fact, if you choose to ingest poison, there's no place on earth that will keep you from dying. You're pretty much doomed.

But when we're talking about *spiritual* life and death, things suddenly become different. Sin is straight-up poison to our souls, and we've all taken a big gulp (see Romans 3:23). By all logic, our collective fate should be sealed. It should be just a matter of time before we keel over before God in judgment. But He was not content to stand by as humanity succumbed to the effects of sin's poison. He intervened directly, carving out a spiritual "living room" in which believers can stand and be safe. This safe space is found in faith in Jesus, and as long as we're standing there, the poison that should have killed us long ago has been rendered useless. It has been nullified by His forgiveness (1 John 1:7).

God is our poison-cancelling refuge—and that's no joke.

 **FOR FURTHER THOUGHT:**

How can a Christian make sure he's standing in God's refuge? Will God let a Christian wander away from safety without warning him?

Lord, thank You for being my remedy—my refuge from the world's toxicity. May I always stand within the safe space of Your protection.

TREASURE

*"The kingdom of heaven is similar to treasure hidden in
a field, which a man found and hid. And for joy over it
he goes and sells all that he has and buys that field."*
MATTHEW 13:44

When most of us think of the "kingdom of heaven," we think
of Revelation's scenes of golden streets, sparkling rivers, and
unending bliss.

But wait—Jesus said in Luke 17:21 that the kingdom of
God is in us *right now*. Clearly then, Jesus' teaching in today's
verse refers to more than simply the afterlife's physical splendor. Rather, He is speaking of the greatest prize of all: God
Himself.

When discussing the tribe of Levi in Deuteronomy
18, God said, "They shall have no inheritance among their
brothers; the LORD is their inheritance" (verse 2). In other
words, their priestly connection with God was worth more
than any physical inheritance in "a land flowing with milk
and honey" (Exodus 3:8).

So if the greatest of all inheritances belonged to Levi's
tribe, then the promise in 1 Peter 2:9—"You are a chosen
generation, a royal priesthood"—means we as Christians are
just as blessed. All the gold and precious jewels that adorn

heaven's streets, though literal, are also a metaphor for the indescribable beauty that comes with a personal, everlasting relationship with our Creator.

Even better, you don't have to wait until you die to experience this. If you're a Christian, then your divine prize is already a part of your life.

Isn't that a treasure worth pursuing?

 **FOR FURTHER THOUGHT:**

Are you satisfied to have God as your treasure? Why
do many people behave as if His glorious presence
is somehow secondary to the gifts He provides?

*Lord, forgive me for not valuing You as highly
as I should. Teach me to see You as the only
treasure worth giving up my life to gain.*

AUTHORITATIVE

How great are His signs! And how mighty are His wonders! His kingdom is an everlasting kingdom, and His authority is from generation to generation.

DANIEL 4:3

Imagine you've stumbled onto a shocking crime scene—a smoking gun, lots of broken glass, and at the center of the room, a lifeless body. What do you do?

First step: contact the authorities.

We trust that no matter what crimes occur—no matter how difficult and perplexing to solve—"the authorities" will have the answer. And usually, we're right. Though the wheels of justice turn slowly, murderers are often apprehended and eventually given a proper sentence. Usually, the victim's family and friends can at least be satisfied that justice was served.

Today's verse declares that God is our ultimate authority. He doesn't need a system of judges and juries to dispense justice. He does all the work Himself, both crafting the laws and upholding them. As a result, whatever He says should be treated as established law—because it is. In fact, Romans 13:1 tells us, "The authorities that exist are ordained by God," so even our earthly authorities must answer to the higher authority who gave them this power.

This also means that whenever we see signs of injustice or evil being committed, we should bring the situation before God, trusting He will act in accord with His righteous character. He already knows the whole situation, and His justice will always come at the perfect time.

God is authoritative whether we admit that or not. Isn't it far better to agree with Him, every time?

 FOR FURTHER THOUGHT:

What do you think when God seems to delay His judgment on evil? What would your life look like had God dished out immediate judgment on you?

Lord, You are the authority of my life—I look to You for guidance, trusting in Your laws and judgments to draw me closer to where You want me to be.

KNOWABLE

"You shall seek Me and find Me,
when you search for Me with all your heart."
JEREMIAH 29:13

Many things in life are simply unknowable, despite our best efforts to understand them. Future events, for instance, will always be shrouded in mystery until they arrive. Then, they'll inevitably lapse back into obscurity as those who experienced them pass away.

Philosophical mysteries as well—such as "What is the nature of the soul?"—are practically unsolvable. And certain scientific pursuits may very well never come to fruition.

With that in mind, isn't it amazing that God—the biggest mystery of all—is knowable to us? We can never know everything about Him...but we can have a personal connection, getting to know Him more each moment we spend in His presence. You're unlikely to ever become friends with the president of the United States, but you are an adopted son of the Creator of all things!

When we search for God, He rewards our inquiry by revealing more truths about Himself—many of which we've discussed in this book. But He gives us more than a mere academic understanding of these attributes. He lets us experience them for ourselves. We become not just knowledgeable of His love and other aspects of His character but recipients of them. We not only believe in God's power, we see it for ourselves.

Today, spend time searching for God—He is knowable for all who seek.

 FOR FURTHER THOUGHT:

Do you crave a deeper understanding of God? What are some ways you can know God on a deeper level? Are you seeking out those avenues of discovery?

Lord, thank You for making Yourself known to me, even though I don't deserve to gain such knowledge. Teach me to search more intently for You.

BEYOND UNDERSTANDING

*O the depth of the riches both of the wisdom and
knowledge of God! How unsearchable are His
judgments and His ways past finding out!*
ROMANS 11:33

Despite the fact that God has made Himself known, there
will always be mysteries about Him. There will always be
things we simply cannot understand: How did He create the
universe from nothing? How does He exist without having
been brought into existence? How does He know the future?
Why does He love us so much?

These are questions that have been tackled by philosophers and theologians throughout history. Yet the outcome
is always the same: the humble admission, "I don't know."
Really, that's the only proper response to God's mysteries. If
He someday chooses to let His children in on His mysteries, what a day that will be! More than likely, however, we
wouldn't understand the answers even if He wrote them on
the side of Mount Everest. Our finite minds weren't built to
grasp the infinite. Only God Himself has that ability.

No matter how deeply philosophers plunge into the
mysteries of existence, their mental picks and shovels will
never scratch the surface of the God who lies beneath it all.

The bedrock of reality doesn't need to explain Himself to mortals—all we need to know is that He loves us and that He is much, much more powerful than we could ever imagine.

 **FOR FURTHER THOUGHT:**

When does legitimate curiosity about God cross the line into arrogance? Do you have a good understanding of just how many things we can't understand about Him?

Mysterious Lord, may I never be so presumptuous to believe I can know everything about You. Show me what I don't know so that I can rejoice in Your superior wisdom.

HIGH PRIEST

In all things it was necessary for Him to be made
similar to His brothers, that He might be a merciful
and faithful high priest in things pertaining to God,
to make reconciliation for the sins of the people.

HEBREWS 2:17

Maybe the job of an Israelite high priest sounds fascinating to you. After all, they were the only ones who were able to approach God directly. What a privilege!

But when you take a closer look at all the requirements a high priest had to meet, this coveted responsibility might lose its appeal. The first and most obvious obstacle would be the purity God required a priest to possess. Leviticus 21 says that any imperfection—physical or spiritual—would lead to automatic disqualification. Uh-oh, there goes about 99 percent of the population. And for the ones who did meet the guidelines, they had to follow instructions to the letter while in God's temple. Otherwise, well, just look at Nadab and Abihu's fate in chapter 10.

Jesus, however, willingly accepted the role of our high priest, and He did so under two outrageous stipulations: He could not sin at all, and He Himself would be the sacrifice. Even the high priests of old were incapable of a sin-free life; rather, they had to purify themselves through sacrifices before approaching God and making sacrifices for others (Hebrews 5:3). Jesus, however, knowing a blameless sacrifice was necessary for the redemption of the world, did things the hard way, fulfilling God's plan of salvation to perfection.

Because of Jesus' willingness to serve, we can approach God any time we want. Make sure you never take that opportunity for granted.

 FOR FURTHER THOUGHT:

Would you qualify to be a high priest in Israel? Why was Jesus willing to undertake such a momentous task?

> *Lord Jesus, I don't deserve any good thing, yet because of Your sacrifice alone, I can stand worthy in Your sight.*

KING

Now to the King eternal, immortal, invisible, the only wise God, be honor and glory forever and ever. Amen.
1 TIMOTHY 1:17

Many people, if they imagined being king, would probably fantasize about wielding the power they've always craved. But even if a king sits in a palace and wears a crown, does that make him a *good* king? Sure, his name will probably appear in history books, but what will these books say about him? Will they consider him a benevolent ruler who loved his people, or will his name become a curse among those who study his reign?

It's been said that good leaders guide people from above, but great leaders lead others from within. Well, God does both. His domain is built on love, and His kingdom consists of human hearts, not land or wealth (Luke 17:20–21). Heaven and earth will one day dissolve, leaving only the souls who've chosen to recognize God as their King. His borders are not physical demarcations—they lie at the edge of belief and loyalty.

And at the end of all things, *everyone* will bow before God as King. For some, it will be enforced upon them, too late for them to enjoy the benefits of knowing Him (Romans

14:11). However those of us who serve Him loyally will be welcomed into His eternal palace, where we will share forever in His reign (2 Timothy 2:12).

God is the only perfect King this world has ever known. Is He reigning in your heart today?

 **FOR FURTHER THOUGHT:**

How can a Christian man honor God as King while still enjoying the personal connection he has with Him? Does God's kingship inspire loyalty or fear in your heart?

> *King Jesus, reign in my heart today.*
> *Be the King of my every passion and*
> *dream. I am Your willing subject.*

MAJESTIC

"Yours, O LORD, is the greatness and the power and the glory and the victory and the majesty, for all that is in heaven and on the earth is Yours. Yours is the kingdom, O LORD, and You are exalted as head above all."

1 CHRONICLES 29:11

In Daniel 4, the arrogant king of Babylon faced a humiliating proclamation from God: Nebuchadnezzar would be driven mad for seven years, roaming the wilderness and feeding on grass like cattle (verses 32–33). The one thing that set him apart as king in the eyes of the people—his majesty—would be stripped away. Such a crushing loss!

As servants of the divine King, we exist solely to proclaim God's majesty. We are His ambassadors (2 Corinthians 5:20), and we are charged with communicating His glory to those living in the kingdom of darkness—a kingdom that will one day be defeated and swallowed up by God's.

But what happens when we as Christians do a poor job of communicating God's majesty? What happens when we preach holiness but live sinfully, proclaiming purity while practicing the opposite? Does this invalidate God's majesty? No, but it hides it from the eyes of those who need to see it.

The world won't want to follow a King whose ambassadors behave more like court jesters. God's majesty will one day be revealed to all. But today it's our job to spread the news of His glory, before it's too late.

 FOR FURTHER THOUGHT:

If you were an unbeliever, how likely would you be to accept Christ if all you saw were the example you're setting now? How can we work to better proclaim God's majesty?

> *Lord, may my actions always reflect Your majesty as King. I never want to hinder the expansion of Your kingdom.*

WISE

To the only wise God be glory forever
through Jesus Christ. Amen.
ROMANS 16:27

Whether you follow the news closely or not, you've probably heard about the rise of artificial intelligence (A.I.)—and the negative impact it could have on humanity. According to the experts, computers may be just a few years away from becoming vastly more intelligent than their human designers—a frightening concept, especially for those science fiction fans who've seen it all before and know what comes next.

Computers can never reach omniscience—that's a property that God alone possesses. But even if they could, they could never attain the wisdom to properly use that knowledge. There is simply no way a mere machine could understand the value of a human life, hence the fear we'd be left with a real-life Terminator.

Thankfully, our God is both all-knowing *and* all-wise. He knows everything that has happened, is happening, will happen, and can happen—and He can change anything He wants at any time. However, because His wisdom is infinite as well, we'll never have to worry about Him abusing this power. The Bible assures us that He always has His children's best interests in mind and actively works to bring about the best possible ending to our stories (Romans 8:28).

Today, be thankful that God is smarter than any machine ever could be—and also infinitely wiser.

 **FOR FURTHER THOUGHT:**

In humans, does intelligence always equal wisdom? Does God's omniscience frighten or reassure you?

All-knowing God, thank You for knowing what is best for me—and for loving me enough to work to bring it about. May I always find solace in Your wisdom.

HELPER

*Behold, God is my helper; the Lord is
with those who uphold my soul.*
PSALM 54:4

If you're like most men, you probably want to appear as strong and intelligent as possible to anyone who may be watching. Some guys take this idea to the point of absurdity.

Trying to haul a couch that's much too heavy? Power through the pain until either the couch reaches its destination or your back gives out. Wrestling with hard emotions and overwhelming grief? Suck up the tears and use them as fuel. Get lost while driving? Refuse to ask for directions and plunge into the wilderness until you run out of gas.

Clearly, too much "strength" can be a weakness in itself. That's why today's verse is so impressive—it shows that King David had managed to overcome this weakness and ask God for help. In fact, he was unapologetic in his admission of helplessness. Many of his psalms revolve around his feelings of confusion, doubt, and fear, and the recognition that only God could bring him through.

And that is exactly what God did, over and over again.

Our God is more than willing to help His children, but only if they are willing to be helped. The moment we adopt the attitude "I can do this myself" is the moment we effectively close ourselves off from our divine helper.

As Christians, we have access to the most powerful being in existence. Why would we ever hesitate to ask Him for help?

 **FOR FURTHER THOUGHT:**

Are you reluctant to ask God for assistance, even when you desperately need it? What steps can a man take to swallow his pride and to reach out for help?

> *Lord, only You can help me in this hard, confusing journey called life. I need Your strength, emotional support, and guidance.*

COMFORTER

"I will pray to the Father, and He shall give you another
Comforter, that He may abide with you forever."
JOHN 14:16

Is there ever such a thing as too much comfort?

That's the question that we, as Christians in a modern, first-world country, should sometimes ask ourselves. Many of us work either from the comfort of our own homes or in the cozy confines of an office cubicle, only to kick back in the evenings in an even more comfortable recliner and eat our favorite comfort foods while watching our favorite comfort shows on television.

And yet, despite all this comfort, it seems people are unhappier than ever. What's behind this paradox?

The answer is found in today's verse. There is only one comforter who can bring true joy, and that is the Holy Spirit. The disciples never knew a fraction of the so-called "comfort" we experience on a daily basis, yet few of us can boast of the level of joy they possessed. Why? Because no matter how much we cram our lives full of shallow comforts, they will only serve to make us feel even more hollow inside if we don't make God our ultimate Comforter. God's comfort stems from His infinite love—His hope that extends far beyond this mundane life on earth.

If we turn to processed foods and mindless entertainment as our source of comfort, we'll inevitably find ourselves dissatisfied and depressed. Only by heeding the Holy Spirit who indwells us can we find a comfort that will never die.

 **FOR FURTHER THOUGHT:**

How can a Christian avoid placing too much stock in shallow comforts? What is a sign that someone values the world's comforts a little too much?

Father, thank You for sending the Comforter into my life. Teach me to rely on Him for my meaning and joy— not on the fleeting pleasures this world calls "comfort."

TEACHER

[Nicodemus] came to Jesus by night and said to Him, "Rabbi, we know that You are a teacher come from God. For no man can do these miracles that You do unless God is with him."

JOHN 3:2

When you were in high school or college, did you ever encounter an instructor who seemed to have one purpose in life: to fail as many students as possible? Each day, this teacher would unload copious amounts of dense information onto the students and assign them impossible amounts of homework. Even worse, whenever someone would ask for help or clarification, the instructor would either ignore the request or give an unhelpful, sarcastic reply. Then, when the test came, the teacher seemed to relish the act of scrawling *F*s with bold, red strokes.

A student could come into such a class passionate about the subject matter—then leave hating it for the rest of his life. Why? Because the teacher's ultimate goal wasn't to teach but to gloat. No teaching was actually accomplished.

Thankfully, that's not the kind of teacher Jesus is. When we enter His classroom, we can expect to learn at the feet of the master teacher who genuinely wants to impart wisdom. Jesus will do everything possible to help His students pass, even going so far as living within us, guiding us every step of the way.

We can choose to reject this teaching, but why would we? Our Lord's curriculum is one of grace and love, and His assignments are easy compared to the burden of sin (Matthew 11:30).

 **FOR FURTHER THOUGHT:**

What are some of the ways Christians can show up in class to receive Jesus' teaching? What has He taught you?

> *Divine teacher, may I never tire of Your spiritual lessons. Keep teaching me what it means to walk in Your love.*

KIND

That in the ages to come He might show the exceeding riches of His grace in His kindness toward us through Christ Jesus.
EPHESIANS 2:7

What does kindness mean to you? Holding the door for a stranger? Paying for another person's meal in the drive-thru? Donating ten bucks to charity on behalf of kids in Africa?

These actions are all wonderful. People who regularly incorporate this kind of behavior into their lives are actively making the world a better place. But none of these things hold a candle to the kindness God has displayed toward His children.

Just as God is infinite in His knowledge, wisdom, power, and love, He is also infinite in His kindness. He is not content with giving us a blessing or two every so often. No, He went so far as to give us the one thing that has infinite value: eternal life, bought with the life of His Son.

We should continue in our quest to be more kind, but the moment we start believing our acts of kindness contribute to our own salvation is the moment we've crossed the line into selfishness again. Our kindness should flow not from our own ambition but from the kindness of God, who lives within us. We'll never reach His level of kindness—nor will we ever fully understand it—but we should actively seek it out, thanking Him regularly and striving to model our lives after the life of Christ.

So, what are you doing with the kindness of God?

 FOR FURTHER THOUGHT:

Does your life display a pattern of kindness?
Besides His death on the cross, in what ways did
Jesus' kindness manifest itself while He was on earth?

> *Lord, there's nothing random about Your acts of kindness—they're perfectly in line with Your character. Teach me to have the same consistency in my acts of kindness.*

GOOD

Teach me to do Your will, for You are my God.
Your Spirit is good; lead me into the land of uprightness.
PSALM 143:10

In C. S. Lewis' first story set in the land of Narnia, *The Lion, the Witch and the Wardrobe*, Mr. Beaver is explaining to the Pevensie children exactly who Aslan is. When he mentions that Aslan is a lion, the young Lucy is surprised. "Then he isn't safe?" Lucy asks. Mr. Beaver replies, "Who said anything about safe? 'Course he isn't safe. But he's good."

The Bible refers to Jesus as "the Lion of the tribe of Judah" (Revelation 5:5), which C. S. Lewis undoubtedly used as inspiration for Aslan's character. But what does this mean for us? After all, we know from the book of Daniel just how unpleasant the prospect of spending a night with lions can be. So why is Jesus compared to one?

Because—like the ferocious king of the jungle—Jesus is entirely beyond our control. His plan for us may lead us to places we'd otherwise never go, and we may start questioning the process along the way. We might even feel helpless—totally at the whim of a greater power whose motives remain mysterious.

Yet because today's verse and many others teach that God

is good, we can entrust our lives to His power.

The mountain pass may be steep and snowy. The swamp might grow dense and deep. But we can trust that the power who led us to that point is the same good power who will lead us through.

 **FOR FURTHER THOUGHT:**

Are you afraid of God's power, or are you trusting in it to guide you home? How has God's power manifested itself in your life?

Lord, because You are good, I place my existence into Your hands, trusting that You'll take me farther than I ever could have traveled on my own.

UNSTOPPABLE

He does according to His will in the army of heaven and among the inhabitants of the earth, and no one can stop His hand or say to Him, "What are You doing?"

DANIEL 4:35

What's the most effective strategy to learn how unstoppable our God is? Just *try* to stop Him. That's what Nebuchadnezzar did, and he immediately learned his lesson—the hard way (Daniel 4:33). Today's verse is his declaration of God's power, after the fact.

Nebuchadnezzar's crash course in learning might be the most effective method, but unless you've gone insane, it's also the worst. There's a far better method, one that involves simply learning from the mistakes of people like the king of Babylon.

Psalm 2 paints a picture of the nations of the earth conspiring together to topple God's reign. What is God's response to this seemingly formidable threat? "He who sits in the heavens shall laugh" (verse 4).

It should be common sense that we mortals can't stop an omnipotent God, but many of us still try. Whenever we do, we're like a chihuahua nipping at the heels of a mighty elephant. God could crush us, in our pitiful arrogance, at any moment—yet He willingly puts up with our foolish defiance, patiently waiting for us to see the error of our ways.

But once it becomes apparent that a man will never learn, all bets are off. It had been better for him if he'd never been born (Matthew 26:24).

When God starts moving, it's time for us to step out of the way—and follow His lead.

 FOR FURTHER THOUGHT:

In what ways is God moving in your life? Are you trying to hinder Him or follow where He leads?

Unstoppable God, may I never try standing in Your way. I want to be on Your side whenever You start to move.

SAVIOR

This is good and acceptable in the sight of God our Savior.
1 TIMOTHY 2:3

When's the last time you saw a movie or read a book in which the protagonist saved the day by putting his own life on the line? Whether it was a superhero flick, an action movie, or a realistic drama, this story probably stirred something deep within your soul, inspiring you to follow the hero's example and dedicate your life to a cause greater than yourself.

But all these stories are plagiarized—they're copied straight from the true story of Jesus that's found in the Bible. Without Jesus' love and sacrifice, our culture would likely be stuck in a cycle of mindless retribution, like the savage empires of old. No matter how much modern society rails against Christians, no one can deny that its moral core—seen so often in the stories that inspire us—has been lifted straight from the pages of scripture.

None of us will ever be able to save a person from sin, yet Jesus calls us to "take up [our] cross" and follow in His footsteps (Matthew 16:24). When we see a need, it's our responsibility to lay down our desires and comforts and confront the need head-on. Jesus was willing to offer His life to save us from the consequences we deserved; we should feel honored to follow in His footsteps in whatever way we can.

Maybe all this post-Christian world needs to see is an honest, real-life emulation of Jesus' saving love.

 **FOR FURTHER THOUGHT:**

In what ways can we be (lowercase) "saviors,"
pointing the world to its ultimate Savior?
How willing are you to sacrifice your comforts for
someone else's spiritual and physical well-being?

> *Lord, this world needs rescuing now more*
> *than ever. May I be willing to play my*
> *part in Your plan to save the world.*

ABOVE ALL

*One God and Father of all, who is above
all and through all and in you all.*
Ephesians 4:6

Many of us love it when life is neat, orderly, and easily com-
partmentalized into lists and hierarchies. There's nothing
wrong with that—in fact, today's verse gives us our first
step toward building our all-important priority list: God is
"above all."

Some Christians read Jesus' warnings against being "of
the world" (John 15:19) as a prohibition of any kind of enjoy-
ment that comes from "secular" pursuits. Hence the existence
of monks and other men and women who cut themselves off
from the world, denying themselves the pleasures of this life
in pursuit of holiness. Others, however, are content with saying, "Jesus comes first," but then living as if He is not even on
their priority list at all.

Neither approach is God's intention for our lives. Paul
warned against cutting ourselves off entirely from the affairs
of this world (1 Corinthians 9:3–10). If we do, how can we
leave a mark on it for Christ? But he also told us to avoid being conformed to our world's twisted morality (Romans 12:2).

The only way this is possible is if we recognize that God

is "above all." When He sits firmly at the top of our priorities pyramid, His teachings and holiness will inevitably trickle down, invading all our activities and passions and pursuits, teaching us to shun what is wicked and embrace what is good.

Because God is above all, we can confidently do all that we do for His glory (1 Corinthians 10:31).

 FOR FURTHER THOUGHT:

Do you recognize God as your number one priority? In what ways does your life show— or maybe fail to show—this attitude?

God, take Your rightful place atop my priorities list. May Your guidance override all the voices crying out from the lower levels of my heart.

THROUGH ALL

*One God and Father of all, who is above
all and through all and in you all.*
EPHESIANS 4:6

"The devil's in the details." You see this phrase crop up whenever a deal that seems too good to be true turns out to be, well, exactly that. Many diabolical scams and schemes have succeeded despite their complete transparency. How? By putting their nasty true intentions into the fine print that nobody reads.

Today's verse, however, offers a much more optimistic spin when it says God is "through all." If the devil lurks in the fine print of online shopping, business transactions, time share properties or anything else we may be involved in, God's presence pervades the fine print of all reality.

When our world seems on the brink of total collapse—when *hope* becomes a dirty word that has no place in our fear-ridden lives—God assures us that He is always operating behind the scenes, pulling the strings to bring about a beautiful ending.

Redemption is hardly ever a straight line—for proof, look no further than the crucifixion. While Jesus' disciples despaired at their Master's untimely death, Jesus was just behind the veil between this life and the next, storming the gates of hell and winning an eternal victory (Matthew 12:29; 1 Peter 3:19). And as the early church struggled under the pressure of persecution, God was ensuring that with every martyr a thousand souls would be inspired to find salvation.

There's no such thing as luck or chance, so remember that no matter how dark this world yet becomes, God is "through all," in every detail.

 FOR FURTHER THOUGHT:

How has God worked through all the events in your life so far? Might your current struggles be yet another stepping stone toward a better future?

Lord, thank You for always working, even when I can't see You. Give me the patience and faith to trust that You are always operating through all.

IN ALL

*One God and Father of all, who is above
all and through all and in you all.*
EPHESIANS 4:6

As we've already discussed, God's kingdom isn't some mystical place like El Dorado or Atlantis—a land far removed from us mortals, reachable only by following a magical treasure map. No, it's *within* us. God's kingdom isn't built from iron and bronze and stone but from love and compassion and grace.

God, as today's verse makes clear, lives inside us. The child of God is truly possessed, not by the forces of darkness but by God's Spirit of light and holiness. He drives our actions, allowing us to exercise our free will yet molding our desires to freely pursue Him.

Of course, this is true not just for us but for all of physical reality. God's presence imbues everything, from the rocks to the trees to the galaxies. This isn't to say our universe is a part of God, like some pantheistic religions teach; rather, it's the other way around—God's presence is a fundamental part of our universe. Without His presence, nothing would exist. Both light and life would cease to be, cut off from God's sustaining power.

If you're struggling to find God through complex rituals and philosophies, stop where you are. He's right beside you, waiting to work within you (Deuteronomy 30:11–14). All He requires is simple faith and surrender.

 **FOR FURTHER THOUGHT:**

When do you feel God's presence most strongly? Are you willing to let Him work in you? If so, what steps have you taken to invite Him in?

> *Lord, You alone permeate all things.*
> *Please invade my life, changing me*
> *from the inside out. Fill me with Yourself,*
> *driving out anything that contradicts Your will.*

EXALTED

"Yours, O LORD, is the greatness and the power and the glory and the victory and the majesty, for all that is in heaven and on the earth is Yours. Yours is the kingdom, O LORD, and You are exalted as head above all."

1 CHRONICLES 29:11

As we've already learned, our God is "above all," and today's verse reiterates that truth. However, it also uses another word to describe God's supremacy.

Exalted is a verb form, implying that someone or something is doing the exalting. But how can this be, since God is, by nature, already above all that exists? Who or what could possibly raise His status any higher? Answer: no one and nothing. What this word means is that God's glory is being made known, not that it's somehow amplified to a greater degree. And who or what is responsible for making God known?

In short, everything—all of creation.

Psalm 19:1 says, "The heavens declare the glory of God," and Jesus boldly proclaims in Luke 19:40, "I tell you that if [My disciples] should remain quiet, the stones would immediately cry out."

Some scientists theorize that our universe is made of

vibrating, extra-dimensional "strings." Whether that's true or not we may never know. But if it is, we can be sure these strings are vibrating to the melody of God's splendor, echoing His song of love and power and redemption through all creation. Our universe is a symphony, and it's playing God's song.

Our job is to join in this divine tune, using the talents God has given us to sing His praises. After all, this life is just a practice run for the worship we'll give Him throughout all eternity.

 ## FOR FURTHER THOUGHT:

In your opinion, in what areas of life is God most highly exalted? In what ways are you exalting God?

Exalted Lord, You are high above all else—may I always realize this truth and strive to give You the recognition You deserve. May my entire life exalt You.

THE WORD

*In the beginning was the Word, and the Word
was with God, and the Word was God.*

JOHN 1:1

Today's verse might be the most profound in the Bible. Within this single sentence is a treasure trove of philosophical complexity—most notably, the notion that Jesus is "the Word."

What does this mean? Isn't the Bible called "the Word"? Clearly, Jesus isn't a book—He is God, and God is a personal being. So why did John speak of Jesus this way?

The answer, surprisingly, can be found in the Greek philosophy of John's day. According to the brightest thinkers of the time, the *logos* (Greek for "word") refers to the divine mind—the rationality and reason—that lies behind all existence. In other words, *logos* is the creative mind of God Himself.

John was apparently fascinated by this idea, so, under the inspiration of the Holy Spirit, he adopted this eloquent term and used it to describe Jesus, Creator of the universe. At the moment of creation, Jesus served as the Father's creative mind and will, dragging existence itself out of the infinite sea of oblivion and kick-starting the history of our world.

As the second person of the Trinity, Jesus is directly responsible for all the beauty we see now (John 1:3). He is not only the Maker of all but also the method and purpose through which the universe came into being (Colossians 1:16–17).

In short, Jesus is the Word, and this Word still desires to communicate His message of love to each of us today.

 **FOR FURTHER THOUGHT:**

How does thinking about Jesus as the Word enrich your understanding of Him? In what ways is God's Word—the Bible—a reflection of His mind as well?

> *Lord Jesus, You are the Word—the creative force behind my life and this world. Teach me to appreciate Your creation as it unfolds exactly the way You have planned.*

ZEALOUS

"Out of Jerusalem a remnant shall go forth,
and those who escape from Mount Zion.
The zeal of the LORD of hosts shall do this."
ISAIAH 37:32

Our God is an extremist.

Okay, that's a loaded word. When we think of extremists, we often think of kamikaze pilots or suicide bombers, bent on the singular goal of hurting others to fulfill their twisted desires. But our God is different. When He came to earth, He knew it was a suicide mission. His life was a ticking bomb, and the prospect of a redemptive death spurred Him on each day. But God's extremism—His zeal—resulted not in the death of innocents but in the pardoning of the guilty.

Jesus went down in a blaze of glory, taking the devil and his accusing power with Him. But that wasn't the end of the story. After Jesus' sacrifice, He exploded from the tomb, triumphantly holding the keys of hell and death (Revelation 1:18). His conquest wasn't just physical—it was a spiritual victory that secured the souls of all who would trust in Him from that time onward.

Yes, *extremist* may be a loaded term, but in light of God's unmatched zeal for the salvation of His children, what other word can we use?

 FOR FURTHER THOUGHT:

Given God's extreme zeal for you, how zealous are you for Him? Are you taking up God's weapons of love and grace? Are you willing to "go down fighting" for righteousness?

> *Lord, I'm through with half-hearted devotion.*
> *Fill me with a burning zeal for Your truth,*
> *just as You are zealous for me.*

ROCK

*He alone is my rock and my salvation. He is
my defense; I shall not be greatly moved.*
PSALM 62:2

God is our rock—this is one of the core teachings repeated throughout the Psalms.

At first, this comparison seems straightforward: God is unmovable, constant, strong—just like a rock. But notice what the psalmist says directly after proclaiming God as his rock: he says, "and my salvation."

Normally, a physical rock doesn't do anything. It just sits there. But here—as well as in other passages like Psalm 28:1—God is portrayed as a rock who actively rescues us and answers prayer.

Is the psalmist simply mixing his metaphors? Highly doubtful. Rather, he's probably referring to an important bit of Old Testament history. In Exodus 17 and Numbers 20, God used a rock to save the Israelites by causing it to produce life-giving water. Centuries later, Paul would proclaim that the Israelites "drank from that spiritual Rock that followed them, and that Rock was Christ" (1 Corinthians 10:4).

In other words, this was a Rock that did more than just sit around. It was active, just like the "rock" in Psalms.

Not only is God our protection from the evil that threatens to chip away at our souls, He is also the source of our strength—the spring of life-giving joy and salvation. God is not an inanimate object; rather, He is actively working in our lives in ways that, by all accounts, should not be possible.

You can take courage and comfort in God, your rock and salvation. He will always defend you.

 FOR FURTHER THOUGHT:

How might today's reading make Moses' punishment (which he received after striking the rock instead of speaking to it) more understandable? How are we sometimes guilty of "striking" God in our impatience?

> *Lord, my rock, please be my defense and my wellspring of strength. Forgive me for the times I have disrespected You or grown impatient with Your timing.*

SHIELD

The Lord is. . .the God of my rock, in Him I will trust.
He is my shield and the horn of my salvation, my high tower
and my refuge. My Savior, You save me from violence.
2 Samuel 22:2–3

David sang today's scripture after God delivered him from Saul's evil schemes. As in yesterday's passage, David says God is his "rock," but this time he also exalts God as his "shield."

Because David was a man of war, his shield metaphor was intended to be taken much more literally than the way we might think of it today. God had protected David from real acts of violence, just like a shield blocking deadly arrows.

For us today, however, David's metaphor becomes even more profound. Just as a shield takes the brunt of a heavy blow, protecting a person from death, so Jesus came to earth with the purpose of becoming our shield. When the darts of our well-deserved punishment were hurtling straight toward our collective throats, Jesus stood in the breach, taking the full wrath of God's judgment on Himself. He allowed us to walk away unscathed.

In short, God did the same thing for David physically that He did for us spiritually on the cross: He saved us from violence. But He went even further, guaranteeing not just our escape from punishment but eternal life in the presence of the God we'd never be worthy to approach on our own.

Jesus is our great shield—are you taking refuge behind Him?

 FOR FURTHER THOUGHT:

What is the process by which a Christian "lifts up" this shield of salvation? In what other ways has God been your shield?

Lord, thank You for being my shield on this spiritual battlefield. May I never forget the continual protection You provide.

DEPENDABLE

And it shall come to pass on that day that the remnant
of Israel, and those from the house of Jacob who have
escaped, shall no longer rely on him who struck them but
shall truly rely on the LORD, the Holy One of Israel.

ISAIAH 10:20

"Keep your friends close but your enemies closer."

This might have been helpful advice for the mafia crew in *The Godfather Part II*, but for the people of Judah, it was a toxic attitude that God wanted them to drop altogether.

Given the number of enemies Judah had, it seemed reasonable for them to lean on other, more powerful nations to protect them from burgeoning threats. There was just one problem, however: the nations they were leaning on hated them just as much as their other enemies did. When Judah leaned on Assyria, for example, Assyria returned the favor by attempting to crush them out of existence.

In other words, keeping their enemies closer than God was a terrible idea.

The forces of evil are fickle and demanding, promising great rewards but then stealing our basic rights. Sin hooks us with guarantees of pleasure, then drops us into a sea of addiction.

Thankfully, we Christians have a better option: God, who saves us from sin. Each time we need help, He steps in and gives us even more than we ask. He is dependable, unlike our enemies.

By keeping God close and our enemies far, far away, we can gain assurance in a world whose promises are only lies.

 FOR FURTHER THOUGHT:

What are some worldly things we Christians sometimes mistakenly trust in? How has God been dependable in your life?

Father, thank You for being a rock-solid source of confidence in this uncertain world. No matter how lost and alone I may feel, Your forgiveness and companionship are only a prayer away.

STRENGTH

*"Behold, God is my salvation. I will trust and not
be afraid, 'for the LORD JEHOVAH is my strength and
my song. He also has become my salvation.'"*

ISAIAH 12:2

When talking about God, we often think of His attributes as qualities He possesses. After all, that's how everything seems to work—a person is either strong or weak, a car is either shiny or dusty, the sky is either clear or cloudy.

But with God, adjectives like *strong* don't begin to describe Him. As we've already learned, God is omnipotent, meaning He not only is strong but possesses *all* strength. In fact, you could even go so far as to say God *is* strength, similar to the proclamation in 1 John 4:8 that "God is love." Whatever attribute God possesses, He possesses it to perfection, making Him the very embodiment of that attribute.

So when today's verse says that God is our strength, it goes beyond a mere statement that our strength comes from God. Rather, God is, quite literally, our strength—the animating force behind our every action. Without His Spirit within us, we'd have no power to choose right from wrong, and without His sustaining power, we'd simply cease to exist. God doesn't just enable us—He *is* our ability.

We should never underestimate God's strength, even in circumstances where we think we have everything under control. We control nothing, and our own strength is non-existent. All power comes from God, and God is all the power we need.

 FOR FURTHER THOUGHT:

Do you regularly thank God for the ability to serve Him? How successful would your Christian walk be if God were not involved?

Lord of strength, please remind me of Your awe-inspiring power whenever I start feeling as if I am somehow strong myself. All my strength is Your strength—so teach me to use it wisely.

MESSIAH

[Andrew] first found his own brother Simon
and said to him, "We have found the Messiah,"
which is, being interpreted, the Christ.
JOHN 1:41

It was an age of oppression for the Israelites. First the Babylonians, then the Persians, then the Greeks, and now the Romans had taken turns plundering and ruling their God-given land. The peace that Jehovah had promised so long ago seemed farther away than ever. Everyone longed for deliverance from this brutal regime.

They longed for a Messiah.

So when Andrew ran to his brother Peter and exclaimed, "We have found the Messiah," his claim went beyond bold and into the realm of audacious. According to popular thought at the time, finding the Messiah meant finding an end to Roman oppression. His announcement was radical, scandalous, treasonous.

And Andrew was right—just not in the way he thought.

While the Jews pined for a warrior Messiah, God was playing the long game. He knew Roman oppression would end soon enough on its own. What His people really needed was salvation from their sins.

The sacrificial system He'd ordained was wearing thin; it had devolved into a set of rituals without a true heavenly connection—a system to be exploited by those seeking power. But then came Jesus, ready to offer His life and put an end not to Roman rule but to the bonds of iniquity itself.

Andrew and Peter didn't realize this at first. How could they? But Jesus' true role as Messiah would soon become apparent, and everything these fishermen had ever known would permanently change.

The Messiah had come, and His new spiritual kingdom would last forever.

 FOR FURTHER THOUGHT:

Are you seeking spiritual deliverance over material deliverance? How will God eventually accomplish both?

Lord, You are my Messiah—my light in this world of darkness. May I never forget the awful fate from which You have rescued me.

SALVATION

*The LORD is my strength and song, and He has become
my salvation. He is my God, and I will prepare Him
a dwelling, my father's God, and I will exalt Him.*
EXODUS 15:2

What does it take to be someone's salvation?

Sometimes, it might mean doing something as simple as
smiling or saying hello to a stranger—unknowingly breaking that person's self-destructive spiral into depression. Other
times, it might mean donating money or clothes or food to a
homeless shelter.

Sometimes, however, the risks are much higher. For instance, a total of 80 firefighters throughout America died in
the line of duty in 2023, and 136 law enforcement officers
met a similar fate.

But God's salvation is different. While we may have
the chance to save a life through our own valiant effort,
Jesus managed to single-handedly offer salvation to the entire world. He was the only one qualified for the job, and the
death rate for this mission was 100 percent.

But so was the success rate.

For everyone who wants to be rescued, the Lord becomes that person's salvation. For those of us trapped in this

burning, sin-riddled world, God's power is our only hope of rescue. And this rescue extends not just to our bodies but to our souls—an eternal salvation that cost God everything, but for us is entirely free.

An unimaginable gift has been offered. Make sure that, by faith, you have accepted it.

 **FOR FURTHER THOUGHT:**

How often do you think of the fate God helped you escape? Is it possible to repay God for His salvation?

Lord, You alone are my salvation. May I follow in Your footsteps, spreading Your love and grace to those who need it, rescuing souls on the brink of perishing.

REDEEMER

*[Jesus] gave Himself for us, that He
might redeem us from all iniquity.*
TITUS 2:14

There are different lenses through which we can view Jesus'
death on the cross. One way it is approached is through the
lens of a legal transaction. Jesus' death sufficed as the payment
for humanity's collective sins, thereby removing the penalty
(*eternal* death) that we would have had to pay. Another
lens is the notion of exemplary love—the idea that Jesus'
death modeled our own obligation to lay down our lives for
our friends (John 15:13).

A third approach is a concept known as *Christus Victor*,
which is taken from such passages as today's. Christus Victor
refers to the idea that we all once carried a price on our
heads—a ransom that, due to our sins, placed us under the
ownership of Satan. The only acceptable ransom would be
the death of a perfect being—the Son of God Himself.

When Jesus died, many believe Satan rejoiced, falsely
thinking his diabolical plan to destroy the Son of God had
worked to perfection. Yes, humanity was freed, but at the cost
of God's Son! This was truly a win for the ages—until, of
course, three days passed and the victorious Messiah burst

from the tomb, robbing the devil of his only triumph.

Jesus is indeed our Redeemer—the one who paid the price no one could pay, buying us back from the sin that enslaved us.

You are no longer a child of evil. You have been redeemed by Goodness Himself. Does your life reflect this truth?

 **FOR FURTHER THOUGHT:**

What are some other ways we can view the atonement? Why is it futile to think we can redeem ourselves from sin?

> *Almighty Redeemer, my fate once lay in the darkness of Satan's kingdom. But now, thanks to You, I can look forward to the beautiful light of heaven. Thank You for this amazing privilege.*

MEEK

*"Take My yoke on you and learn from Me, for I am meek
and lowly in heart, and you shall find rest for your souls."*
MATTHEW 11:29

Today's verse reveals that Jesus is meek—a word that doesn't usually bring any God-like attributes to mind. After all, aren't meek people generally pushovers, unwilling to stand up for themselves or against injustice?

To the world, yes. But for Jesus there's an infinite gap separating the words *meek* and *weak.*

Nobody knows who first coined the saying, "The strength in power is knowing when not to use it," but this message can be seen throughout the Bible. In Matthew 26:53, Jesus says that He had the power to call "twelve legions of angels" to fight on His behalf, rescuing Him from an awful death on the cross. In fact, since He was God incarnate, this was an understatement: He could have destroyed the universe and started a new one—all with a single thought.

But He didn't.

Even now, as the world blasphemes His name and opposes His plan, Jesus has the power to destroy everything in a divine inferno, melting the very elements into oblivion (2 Peter 3:12).

But He doesn't.

Why? Because even though Jesus is all-powerful, He currently chooses meekness over strength, gentleness over aggression, redemption over wrath. One day, Jesus will come not as a lamb but as a lion. But until that day, this world is spared by the meekness of the Son of God.

 FOR FURTHER THOUGHT:

Are you striving to live like Jesus, replacing anger with meekness? What would your life be like if Jesus hadn't been meek toward you?

Lord Jesus, You show meekness toward a world that seems bent on provoking Your wrath. I myself was once among their ranks, but Your gentleness saved me. Thank You.

GLORIFIED

"I will be sanctified in those who come near Me,
and before all the people I will be glorified."
LEVITICUS 10:3

Merriam-Webster defines the word *glorious* as "marked by great beauty or splendor." So in this context, how does it define *glorify*? Simple: "to give glory to (as in worship)."

As we've already learned, God is exalted whether people choose to exalt Him or not. The same holds true for the word *sanctified* in today's verse—God is already holy; He does not need anybody to designate Him as such. God is already glorified. He not only possesses "great beauty" and "splendor"— He is the epitome of these qualities. No amount of praise will increase His level of glory. Yet we're still obligated to give Him the glory He deserves.

Why? Because God created us as incomplete creatures— cavity-filled souls that will inevitably collapse on themselves in the absence of outward-facing praise. The moment we stop glorifying God is the moment we start directing that glory toward our own souls, imploding ourselves in the process and robbing our lives of their sole true purpose.

In other words, we either glorify God or perish spiritually—this truth is built into our very nature. God deserves each ounce of praise we can offer Him (and more), so He made the act of praise as necessary for us as water.

God *will* be glorified—it's up to us whether we want to join in this everlasting chorus.

FOR FURTHER THOUGHT:

In what ways does your life glorify God? In what ways might it be glorifying you? How can you repurpose those areas so that they point back toward Him?

> *God of glory, I want to glorify Your name—*
> *now and forever. Teach me to reject*
> *self-worship in favor of selfless praise.*

INVITING

The Spirit and the bride say, "Come." And let him
who hears say, "Come." And let him who is thirsty come.
And whoever desires, let him take the water of life freely.
REVELATION 22:17

God isn't in the business of forcing people to do anything. He created this world as a place where humanity could be free to choose—a testing ground for embodied souls.

Of course, God *could* force everyone on earth to bend a knee right now and worship Him, but would this really be worship? Such a world would be a planet of puppets, robbed of their own voice and given their words by a cosmic ventriloquist. Just as a robot programmed to say, "I love you" could never be truly loving, so mandatory worship would make true worship impossible. Authentic praise cannot exist without the sense of awe and gratitude that inspires it.

In other words, God does not put words in our mouths. Rather, He simply gives us a reason to say them.

Today's verse expresses this truth. The wedding feast has been prepared, and the last echoes of God's invitation are still ringing through history. When will this call fade to silence and the gate forever be shut? We won't know until it happens. All we know is that for today, the call still stands.

God has given you every reason to come and join Him. Have you answered the call?

 **FOR FURTHER THOUGHT:**

How can the fact that we have free will be both liberating and frightening? How are you exercising your ability to choose?

Lord, I won't wait another day to answer Your call—not only toward heaven but toward a richer, more fulfilling walk with You.

VINDICATOR

"I will accept [Job], lest I deal with you according
to your folly, in that you have not spoken of Me
the thing that is right, like my servant Job."
JOB 42:8

In case you haven't noticed, there are a lot of competing views about who God truly is. Some say He's a God of hatred and revenge, commanding His followers to commit acts of violence against "infidels." Others lie on the opposite end of the spectrum, claiming God is so lenient that He is willing to overlook the sins even of those who actively oppose Him. Still others believe Him to be a small-*g* god—a Zeus-like caricature, an old man in the clouds. Many more will say God is inseparable from the universe. Others deny His existence altogether.

Clearly, all of these can't be true at once. God is not a figment of our imagination—His existence and character correspond to the truth, not to our notions of what we think the truth should be. That's why He gave us His Word—to reveal the truth to us mortals, who'd never figure it out on our own.

While we live on this planet, God mercifully waits for those who spew false doctrine to repent and recognize His true nature. He wants nothing more. But for those who don't,

God will serve as vindicator—both of His own nature and of all the faithful who preached His Word. All wrong, harmful doctrine will be eternally corrected, and everything true will stand with Him forever.

 FOR FURTHER THOUGHT:

When Jesus returns, will you be vindicated, or will God vindicate the ones you oppose? How can a Christian make sure he's always in the first group?

> *Lord, You have an astounding sense of justice— even Your enemies will one day declare their punishment is just. May I never try to vindicate myself but instead trust Your judgment.*

AUTHOR

Looking to Jesus, the author and finisher of our faith.
HEBREWS 12:2

When we think of God as an author, the first thing that comes to mind is probably the Bible, His Word. After all, 2 Timothy 3:16 says, "All scripture is given by inspiration of God."

But this analogy goes even deeper. Today's verse, for instance, says Jesus is the author of salvation—meaning that God's plan of redemption was written before the world began. . .then enacted to perfection on the cross. Just as a brilliant play is authored by a brilliant mind, so the brilliant plan of salvation was imagined by the most brilliant mind of all. But for God's story of salvation, no revision process was necessary: He got it perfect the first time.

But there's another sense in which God can be seen as an author. It's been said that the word *history* can be split into two words, "His story," with *His* referring to God. Passages like Proverbs 16:33—which says, "The lot is cast into the lap, but the decision-making is of the LORD"—certainly support this notion. It's not that God has robbed us of our free will. Rather, He knew what we'd freely choose before we even had the chance to choose, and He placed us in our designated spots in history accordingly. We are free agents, in other words, but we're simultaneously living out the story God has already written. We're live actors in His cosmic drama.

Only He knows how the story ends—it's up to us to simply be faithful.

 **FOR FURTHER THOUGHT:**

How can thinking of God as author be liberating
for the believer who seeks to do His will?
Which side of God's story are you on?

> *Lord, use me as a quill pen to write my*
> *small portion of Your grand book. I want*
> *to be a part of Your living story.*

OWNER OF ALL

"For every beast of the forest is Mine,
and the cattle on a thousand hills."

PSALM 50:10

According to the Madison Trust Company, the award for the most land owned goes to King Charles III and the British royal family. The scale of their property is massive—a whopping 6.6 billion acres, or about a sixth of the planet's total surface area. Coming in second is the Roman Catholic Church, with close to 0.2 billion acres.

That's a lot of land! Yet in light of today's verse, these impressive numbers are just fictional figures—none of it really belongs to anyone other than God.

Sure, these people may have acquired the land, but God was the one who created it and upholds it by His power. Not only that, He also owns the land on every other planet in the cosmos—as well as all the space between them. The whole universe is God's—not a human alive truly owns a single square inch.

Instead, He has entrusted us as stewards of this land, caretakers charged with preserving His creation. This isn't a pagan, New Age concept—it's biblical, reaching back into the second chapter of Genesis (verse 15). We dare not worship this earth, but we *should* worship the one who made it—and one way of worshipping Him is by appreciating the things He created for us to enjoy.

Your house, your land, your car, your family, and even you—all of it belongs to God. How do you view and use His resources?

🔆 FOR FURTHER THOUGHT:

What does misusing God's resources look like? What goal should we have when it comes to utilizing our possessions?

> *Lord, owner of all, show me how to use the resources You've allowed me to borrow. I want to employ them in a way that will advance Your kingdom, not fulfill my selfish desires.*

SUCCESSFUL

"God is not a man, that He should lie, nor the son of man,
that He should repent. Has He said, and shall He not do
it? Or has He spoken, and shall He not make it good?"

NUMBERS 23:19

Frustration usually arises whenever there is a gap between what we want to do and what we can actually accomplish. The moment we find out our valiant efforts have been in vain, we humans become acutely aware of the time we wasted chasing an unobtainable goal.

God, however, is immune to all such weaknesses. The moment He sets out to perform a task, it's already done. To us, it may appear as if His plan has failed or is taking too long, but God doesn't see the world as a progression of unfolding events—He sees all times all at once. The end of His plan, in other words, is simultaneous with its beginning. His success rate is 100 percent.

Of course, this is not to say that God remains aloof from the bad happenings on this planet. After all, John 3:16 says that God wants the entire world to be saved—an outcome that, sadly, will never happen. What God's successfulness does mean, however, is that He is able to use negative events to accomplish His ultimate goals. Since God doesn't interfere with our free will, He arranges things so that our free will leads to the outcome He devised.

He's the master chess player, in other words, and His "checkmate" has already been declared.

 FOR FURTHER THOUGHT:

In what ways has God used negative events in your life to achieve positive outcomes? Why do you think God made humans incapable of seeing the future?

Lord, I don't see how my current situation can be part of Your plan. But that's okay—I never see the big picture until it arrives. Thank You for ensuring the success of all who trust in You.

BUILDER

For he looked for a city that has foundations,
whose builder and maker is God.
HEBREWS 11:10

"In the beginning God created the heaven and the earth" (Genesis 1:1).

This simple sentence begins the scriptures, and establishes God's role as the ultimate architect. The whole of reality, created in a single instant of divine strength—that's how awesome God's creative power is.

When Jesus came to earth, it's fitting that out of all the occupations that existed at the time, He became a carpenter (Mark 6:3)—someone who builds for the good of others. The one who'd built reality with a single thought now labored in flesh and blood with dusty tools to build houses and furniture and other useful things. But during this time, Jesus was also building something greater, something created not from wood and stone but from instruction and love—He worked to build God's kingdom. And then, as the barbaric Romans hung Jesus on the cross, maliciously using the very type of instruments He'd used all those years to help others, Jesus built our salvation. Its blueprints were written in His blood, and He followed the project through with His obedience.

And then, Jesus rose from the tomb, beginning a new building project that is mentioned in today's scripture. The completion date for this heavenly city is yet to be announced, but given that the one who instantly created the universe has been preparing it for us for the past two thousand years (John 14:2), it's guaranteed to be spectacular.

 **FOR FURTHER THOUGHT:**

How eager are you to see the place Jesus is preparing for you? Why? What do you expect it to be like?

> *God, I'm in awe at the material cosmos and the spiritual kingdom You have built, so I can only imagine what heaven will be like. I can't wait to see the finished product.*

MEDIATOR

For there is one God and one mediator between
God and men, the man Christ Jesus.
1 Timothy 2:5

Have you ever tried calling the headquarters of a relatively large corporation, seeking to "speak to a representative"? If so, the chances are high that you were never able to speak to an actual person. It seems all the "representatives" were robots, programmed with an okay understanding of the English language but lacking any real connection to you, the caller.

In other words, the larger the company, the harder it is to speak to a flesh-and-blood mediator. And it's even harder to find someone who's actually invested in the company's goals.

Jesus, however, is the perfect mediator between God and man. Why? Because Jesus is the "express image" of God Himself—the second person of the Trinity. When you call on the Father and Jesus answers, it's as if you're speaking to the Father directly.

Jesus won't transfer your call to voicemail or refer you to a less-experienced heavenly citizen, nor will His primary goal be ending the call as soon as possible. No, He genuinely cares about the quality of your relationship with God—so much so, in fact, that He gave His life to make it possible.

How's that for a great representative?

 **FOR FURTHER THOUGHT:**

When you pray, do you think about Jesus' role as mediator?
How might dwelling on this truth give you a better
understanding of the Trinity and its significance for us?

> *Father God, may I never hesitate to ask You*
> *for anything—I know You and Your Son are*
> *always pleased to hear from Your children.*
> *I'm grateful for Jesus' constant intercession.*

ANCHOR

By two immutable things, in which it was impossible
for God to lie, we who have fled for refuge to take hold
of the hope set before us might have a strong consolation.
We have this hope as an anchor for the soul, both sure and
steadfast, and which enters into that within the veil.

HEBREWS 6:18–19

Thalassophobia—"fear of the sea."

Maybe you've heard of this condition before. Perhaps you might even have it. It's not the most common phobia, but there's probably not a sailor alive who hasn't looked out at the vastness of water surrounding him and never felt even a small twinge of fear. And rightfully so—the ocean is huge and dark and deep. Monsters straight out of horror tales live in its depths, waiting to feast on the bones of the careless and unlucky.

That's why anchors are so important: they prevent ships from drifting too far from land and becoming bait for the nameless creatures of the deep.

Today's verse says that God's perfection and His inability to lie serve as our anchor in this ocean of fear. In the middle of sickness, persecution, disease, and even death, God is our grounding weight—our anchor that keeps us from helplessly drifting into the oblivion of anxiety and despair.

If you haven't cast out your anchor yet, do it now, while you still have sight of land.

 **FOR FURTHER THOUGHT:**

At what point in your life did you feel the most lost and alone? Did you continue clinging to God during that time? Why is letting go of God the worst thing a Christian can do?

Lord, even when all my earthly security has come undone, You are the one anchor that grounds my soul to peace. Keep holding my life, enabling me to resist the destructive tide of doubt.

BLESSED

Blessed be the Lord, who daily loads us with
benefits, even the God of our salvation.
PSALM 68:19

Have you ever thought of what it means for God to be
"blessed"? Whenever God pours out His blessings on us, we
experience a small fraction of His infinite power. The snow
in His treasuries and the forces of lightning and hail and
wind and rain pour endlessly from the God who stores them
within His grasp (Job 38:22–30).

Even more, all the love and grace and peace and joy we
experience come as a result of God's own attributes overflow-
ing into our lives, blessing us with a fraction of a fraction of
the perfection that belongs to God.

In other words, when we call ourselves blessed, having
received such a small portion of the things God has eternally
owned, how much more blessed is the God who gave them?

In addition to the sheer scale of God's blessedness, the
main thing that separates His blessings from ours is the fact
that while we rely on Him for our blessings, He relies on
nobody but Himself. His blessedness is an intrinsic part of
His nature. "Blessed be the Lord" is an act of worship that we,
His blessed children, offer as praise.

If you seek blessings, don't look to the world or even to yourself—look to the God who holds infinite blessings in His hand and is always willing to give to those who ask.

🔅 FOR FURTHER THOUGHT:

What are some basic blessings in your life? How does God always make sure even the "poorest" Christians among us have something to praise Him for?

> *Blessed God, You are glorious and blessed beyond comprehension. May I use the blessings You have given as tools to worship You.*

WITH US FOREVER

"Behold, I am with you always, even to the end of the world."
MATTHEW 28:20

It's been said that hell is marked by the absence of God, complete with the suffering that comes from being separated from His presence. If so, then it follows that for those of us who believe—and are thus rescued from hell—we will never have to experience the pain of God's absence. No matter where we go, how hopeless the future looks, or how painful our losses become, God will always be with us—from now through eternity.

So what does this mean for us? First, it means that fear is irrational. Imagine walking on a sturdy glass bridge over the Grand Canyon, seeing the canyon walls stretching thousands of feet below you. Your first instinct may be fear, but it's an irrational fear, divorced from the reality of the protection offered by the bridge. Similarly, since God's presence is sometimes transparent, we see danger all around but are shielded from its harmful effects. Even when the world is on fire with chaos and despair, we are resting safely in God's presence.

Second, it means our future will always be brighter than where we are today. Whether you're coasting on the breeze of riches and good health or battling uphill through poverty and shame, as long as you keep trusting God, you are assured an eternal home with Him—a world with neither pain nor our tendency toward pride and self-reliance.

Jesus is with us, now and forever. What other reason for rejoicing do we need?

 FOR FURTHER THOUGHT:

If God is always with us, why does it sometimes feel like He is not? What do you do in these times? What *should* we do?

Thank You, Jesus, for being with me always. Alone, I'd have lost my way so long ago. But with You as my guide, I'm certain I'll reach heaven someday.

ALL YOU NEED

And He said to me, "My grace is sufficient for you,
for My strength is made perfect in weakness."
Therefore, I will boast most gladly even more in my
weaknesses, that the power of Christ may rest on me.

2 CORINTHIANS 12:9

John D. Rockefeller, once the richest man in the world, was famously asked by a reporter, "How much money is enough?" His response: "Just a little bit more."

This snappy, humorous reply holds the secret of the ubiquitous dissatisfaction that festers in the heart of humanity. We're all hungry creatures, craving what we cannot have. Or if we do reach our goals, we create new, even more audacious ones so we can crave those instead. Craving is built into our DNA, making earthly satisfaction impossible.

But notice the word *earthly*. Why would God, our loving Creator, build us in such a way that our hopes and dreams could never be realized using the resources He gave us? Because He wants us to remember the reason we exist in the first place—to serve and worship Him forever (Ecclesiastes 12:13). As a result, no amount of money or pleasure or fame or power or influence or comfort or security or earthly joy can fill the infinite, God-shaped void inside your soul.

God has created us with desires that reach beyond the physical. And once we have Him, all other lesser cravings will effortlessly slip away.

God is all you need.

 ## FOR FURTHER THOUGHT:

How can a Christian keep from viewing the blessings God has given us as a source of ultimate satisfaction? Are you dissatisfied with your life or is having God enough?

> *Lord, Your love and grace are all I need, and that's exactly what You give. My search for meaning and fulfillment ends here, in Your presence.*

The Trusted King James Version. . .
Just Easier to Read

God Is. . .All You Need quotes scripture from the
Barbour Simplified KJV. Maintaining the familiarity
and trustworthiness of the King James Version,
it removes the difficulties of antiquated language
and punctuation. Keeping all the original translation
work of the 1611 Bible, the Barbour Simplified KJV
carefully updates old styles that may interfere with your
reading pleasure and comprehension today.